SEEKING GOD'S PEACE
IN A NUCLEAR AGE

A Call to Disciples of Christ

Seeking God's Peace in a Nuclear Age

A Call to Disciples of Christ

CBP Press
St. Louis, Missouri

Library of Congress Cataloging in Publication Data

"Prepared at the request of the general minister and president of the Christian Church (Disciples of Christ)"
Bibliography: p. 91.
Includes index.
1. Peace—Religious aspects—Christianity. 2. War—Religious aspects—Christianity. 3. Nuclear warfare—Religious aspects—Christianity. I. Christian Church (Disciples of Christ)
BT736.4.S44   1985   2411.6242   85-7836

ISBN: 0-8272-3422-8

Scripture quotations, unless otherwise noted, are from the Revised Standard Version of the Bible, copyrighted 1946, 1952, © 1971, 1973 by the Division of Christian Education of the National Council of the Churches of Christ in the U.S.A. and are used by permission.

Printed in the United States of America

Prepared at the Request of
the General Minister and President
of the Christian Church (Disciples of Christ)

Foreword

The Christian Church (Disciples of Christ) has declared "the pursuit of peace with justice" as a priority.

Though Disciples of Christ have not been a traditional "peace church," we have called upon our people to make responsible Christian judgments concerning issues of war and peace.

The nuclear age has introduced new dimensions to the ethics of war, the full implications of which are just now emerging for most of us. The questions being raised cannot be answered by the traditional solutions we have used.

Believing that the church has a responsibility to provide for its members guidance for their ethical thinking, I appointed a Panel on Christian Ethics in a Nuclear Age, made up of able and respected persons, to reflect upon those issues and to share with the membership of the church the results of that reflection.

A first draft of their work was shared with a widely representative group of several hundred persons with the request that they review it and give the Panel their reactions. The document has now been revised and is being issued by the Panel not as a policy statement of the Church, but as "A Call to Disciples of Christ" to explore the moral and ethical questions we face. Though prepared principally for Disciples, we offer it to the public at large as a contribution to all who are "Seeking God's Peace in a Nuclear Age."

Kenneth L. Teegarden
General Minister and President
Indianapolis, Indiana
1985

Seek peace, and pursue it.

Psalm 34:14

Blessed are the peacemakers.

Matthew 5:9

Let us then pursue what makes for peace
and for mutual upbuilding.

Romans 14:19

For he is our peace, who has made us both one,
and has broken down the dividing wall of hostility. . . .
And he came and preached peace.

Ephesians 2:14, 17a

CONTENTS

Introduction

The Panel's Task

1)   The prospect of nuclear war oppresses millions of people today. Before this new and terrible possibility, old modes of defense and traditional patterns of thinking on the ethics of warfare all seem insufficient. Yet the conviction that we must act in faithfulness in the attempt to save our world from incineration and ourselves from involvement in an act of unspeakable savagery possesses the Christian conscience. The obligation of preventing a nuclear holocaust weighs heavily upon us. What then ought we to do? The question concerns people in every walk of life and of all ages.

2)   To guide the members of the Christian Church (Disciples of Christ) in engaging this fateful question, the General Minister and President, with the encouragement of the Administrative Committee of the General Board, early in 1983 convened a Panel on Christian Ethics in a Nuclear Age. This Call to Disciples of Christ comes out of the Panel's work, carried on in dialogue with concerned persons, across a period of two years. Having no mandate to speak officially for our church, the Panel intends to offer a Christian witness to the church. At the same time we hope to involve many in such reflection on the issues as will lead them to their own firm stand as Christians, not merely in the privacy of personal opinion but in the arena of public policy.

3)   Our method of work as a Panel has involved us in a process which we commend to others, whether studying alone or working in groups. We therefore invite our readers to confront the nuclear reality in all its starkness, as we have done, explor-

ing the Christian heritage for the resources it offers in dealing with the threat, and choosing those courses of action which they themselves consider most in keeping with the Christian calling to be peacemakers. We have not shirked our responsibility to make the hard choices. On each of the major options for dealing with nuclear weapons, the Panel clearly states the position to which it has come and the reasons for its decision.

4)   The Panel's work has not gone on in isolation. We have carefully considered the deliberations of scientists, military analysts, journalists, and other students of the issues, giving particular attention to the work of ecumenical and denominational groups. We solicited opinions by questionnaire from all participants in the General Assembly of the Christian Church (Disciples of Christ) meeting at San Antonio, Texas, in 1983 and by a request in the church press. We have read and analyzed 952 replies to the questionnaire, as well as scores of letters. In the summer of 1984 we sent copies of our preliminary draft to hundreds of persons within and beyond our church, carefully selected in an effort to secure comments from representatives of specific concerns and areas of expertise. Many of these responded, some with brief observations on a particular point, others with extended and careful analysis of our draft. A college class spent several weeks in developing a meticulous commentary. A minister's widow past ninety years of age wrote to express appreciation that her church is dealing with the nuclear issue in this way. These contributions materially aided the Panel in preparing this final form of our address to the church.

5)   While the Panel gladly offers its work to all who are attempting to avert the threat of nuclear destruction, we have kept clearly in mind our mandate to address the Christian Church (Disciples of Christ). Because we speak out of the tradition of this church and to its people, our document has a distinctive character, which we do not, however, intend as sectarian. Grateful for the extensive literature of high quality on the nuclear issue, on much of which we have drawn as indicated in the Notes and Resources for Study, we have attempted neither to duplicate nor to supplant that literature. Ours has been a more modest goal: to guide our church in a responsible approach to the issues through ways of reflection characteristic of our heritage as Disciples of Christ. Other persons to whom such ways of thinking commend themselves may also find help in

our work. If so, we are grateful, for our common humanity makes allies of us all in the effort to prevent nuclear annihilation.

6)   Because ours is a church made up of congregations in the Dominion of Canada and the United States of America, we have kept our focus on decisions which must be made by the citizens of these two nations, who bear ultimate responsibility for public policy there. And inasmuch as only one of our two nations is a nuclear power, a number of the specifics with which we must deal pertain only to it. While we believe that the course of action we commend to our peoples and leaders is one which should be followed everywhere, we have not undertaken to exhort the citizens or governments of other continents. We trust that in a common concern for peace they too will be moved to a similarly responsible and constructive course of action.

An Overview

7)   Our document contains four chapters, arranged to a large degree in the order in which the Panel did its work.

8)   We begin with an account (Chapter I) of the church's efforts in the past to come to terms with the problems which war presents to the Christian conscience. We deal with pacifism in the early church and in more recent times, indicating why some Christians as a matter of conviction have refused to engage in war, and raising questions which such a position naturally calls to mind. We present the doctrine of the just war and its standards, noting that it requires Christians to form a moral judgment respecting any war in which their nation may be engaged. We recall the mentality of the Crusades and the temptation to regard the foes of the nation as enemies of God. We observe the need to assess anew the usefulness of these theories, particularly with reference to nuclear war.

9)   Next we move to the distinctive heritage of Disciples of Christ, beginning with their vision of freedom, justice, and peace. We note a constant insistence on moral integrity and social service, along with a persistent involvement with issues of public policy. Chief among these has been a concern for peace. Yet Disciples have seldom taken a unanimous stand regarding

13

any particular question, having been influenced more than they realized by assumptions prevalent in their own time and place. They have nevertheless followed a characteristic approach to public issues, an approach which is scriptural, pragmatic, and reasonable, with a high regard for freedom of opinion, yet insistent on taking into account the common mind of the Christian world and on consulting with other people of goodwill. To the extent that Disciples have escaped from the sentiment of the moment to reach a considered Christian position, they have done so by using the approach just indicated. Disciples are now called to deal in Christian faithfulness with the issues of the nuclear age.

10)   The changing nature of warfare and the immeasurable destructiveness of nuclear weapons provide the substance of Chapter II. Our historical survey points out a persistent linkage binding economic expansion with the enhancement of military power and these two with political advantage, a union which has now appropriated technology into the linkage. The result is nuclear weaponry. It threatens not only the armies of the enemy, but millions of civilians as well. It threatens not only the populations of targeted areas, but those whom these weapons are intended to defend. It threatens not only the citizens of the powers waging nuclear war, but millions of others who are not party to the conflict, as winds and waters carry radioactive dust over the earth. It threatens not only the human inhabitants of this planet, but many other living creatures, perhaps even every form of life and the very possibility of life for untold ages. The facts are commonly known, but we have gathered those we consider most crucial.

11)   Our assignment was handed to us as Christians. Consequently we ask in Chapter III what particular resources the Christian heritage offers those who seek to make peace and to prevent nuclear war. We deal first with the biblical vision of *shalom*, God's promise of harmonious unity throughout creation and especially in the whole human family, a unity growing out of justice and issuing in peace; by the sacred covenant which God has given, believers are bound to God to serve in actualizing that biblical dream. Next we take up some basic themes of Christian faith, exploring the implications of our most elemental confessions ("I believe in God, in Jesus the Christ, in the Holy Spirit") for our call to become active peace-

14

makers. Then we move on to the essentials of Christian ethics. We set forth ways in which Christians responsibily determine issues of right and wrong, giving special attention to considerations which bear on questions of nuclear policy.

12)   So we come in Chapter IV to the specifics of making peace in a nuclear age. We present the obligation of individual Christians and of the church as a body to deal with a public issue as compelling as nuclear war and suggest ways in which that mission may most faithfully be fulfilled. We examine the major options now being proposed for preventing such a conflict and suggest questions which must be raised in each case. The climate of international relations seems to have moderated slightly since the Panel began its work, and it could change rapidly again, for better or for worse, by the time this document reaches the churches. Yet despite fast-breaking developments in the news, the major options we discuss seem likely to remain relevant for some time to come. On each of these controversial topics the Panel indicates in boldfaced type the conclusion we have reached during our two years of study and the reasoning which underlies that conclusion. We press upon each of our readers the urgency of coming to a personal judgment as a Christian on the best way of preventing nuclear war and then of translating that judgment into action. Accordingly, we close our document with a Call to Commitment.

A Call to Study, Dialogue, and Action

13)   The careful reader will note a recurrence of certain themes at various points within our document. This is not due to thoughtless repetition. Rather, the Panel deliberately takes up again in a new context an emphasis previously considered so that it may be further developed and applied in a new way. In the most important instances of this kind a note within parentheses refers to earlier discussions of the theme in question.

14)   The Panel believes that responsible Christian action regarding the issues of nuclear war requires study, information-sharing, ethical thinking, and dialogue, within the fellowship of the church, and beyond. We look upon our Call, however, as far more than a study document. Rather, we see it as a guide for

15

Christian minds engaged with hard choices in a time of peril for all humanity. We offer this statement as our contribution to the dialogue and commend it to you for your response in thought and faithful action.

I. War and the Christian Conscience

15)   The issues of nuclear warfare bewilder and divide Christians. It may throw light on our confusion if we reflect on how we came to the place where we are. As we examine Christian attitudes toward war and peace through the long sweep of church history, we discover that the differing and sometimes opposite points of view did not necessarily result from intentional reflection on the gospel; sometimes they mirrored the assumptions of the society in which they arose or even the lingering influence of other cultures. This is true of the classical formulations of the early Christian centuries. It is also true of the thinking of Disciples of Christ in the nineteenth and twentieth centuries.

A. *Classical Christian Options*

16)   In the beginning, the church was not recognized as a legitimate, organized religious body and had no way of addressing governmental issues in an autocratic Roman empire. Because Christians refused to engage in the ceremony of allegiance to the emperor, which involved the worship of pagan gods, they could not hold public office. When in A.D. 311 Constantine and his colleagues issued an edict of religious toleration, the church emerged out of a three-hundred-year exclusion from politics. Now it began to develop an ethic of public involvement. That thinking drew on the entire body of scripture —not only the New Testament, but the Law and the Prophets, the Psalms and the Wisdom Literature—as well as on the principles of classical philosophy. This meant that the developing Christian ethic of war was not unique to Christians. It was worked out within a context heavily influenced by Hebrew, Greek and Roman thought.

17)   Overall, the church has developed three different positions on war and peace: pacifism, the just war theory, and the notion of a crusade. Although the three emerged in the order listed, they have sometimes existed side by side. At various times, one has prevailed over the others.

1. Pacifism

18)   Up to the time of Constantine (A.D. 313) the early church was predominantly pacifist. Although pacifism has had many different meanings down through the ages, it is in essence a principled objection to taking the life of another, serving in the military, and waging war. In the early church it tended to accompany an attitude of withdrawal from worldly life. Because the church was an outlawed minority and since Christians could not swear a pagan oath of loyalty to Caesar, there was little involvement in any aspect of government or politics.

19)   The early church was not absolutist in its pacifism, however; some soldiers continued to serve in the army after their conversion to Christianity and they were not excluded from communion. The dominant attitude nevertheless restrained most early Christians from military service.

20)   The convictions which led Christians to accept pacifism have varied with the times. In the early church, the outright rejection of war may have been less determinative than the fear of idolatry. Yet destruction of human life in war seemed to usurp a right belonging to God alone. Christians were fearful of supporting a state or any earthly power which rivaled the sovereignty of God. The outstanding characteristic of the medieval pacifists was a return to the Bible, supremely the Sermon on the Mount, as their primary rule. For them nonviolence was the law of Christ. In the Reformation era, among Anabaptists and others, the "emphasis was upon suffering, the necessity for suffering, in the Christian ethic." For Quakers and other members of historic peace churches in this country, "a new respect for personality and a new faith in the capacities of man" proved decisive.[1] Acknowledging the dignity of persons brought many to this form of pacifism, and not a few Christian humanists advocated this position. Alexander Campbell derived his doctrine of pacifism, like his position on baptism, from his study of the New Testament. Pacifism today is a minority movement in most churches. It often takes the form of conscientious objection to

war and nonviolent civil disobedience intended to effect basic reforms toward social justice. For many it is a way of living—understanding, reconciling, mutually succoring, loving, making friends and not enemies.

21)   Because of the varying convictions which have supported a pacifist witness, different attitudes result. Some are negative, involving a passive stance, as, for example, the early Christians in their withdrawal from society, or David Lipscomb, patriarch among the Churches of Christ, who held that a Christian should not vote or hold civil office. For others, pacifism has meant an active participation in political decision-making rather than a sectarian stance of cutting all ties with the world. Disciples like F. D. Kershner and Kirby Page represented such a pacifism of involvement in social change. It is an absolute that derives its conviction "not from the negative abhorrence of war nor from the utopian dream of a lotus-eater's world, but from the fact and significance of Jesus Christ."[2] From the early church down to the present, pacifists of diverse outlooks have borne their witness, though most of the time only as a prophetic and provocative minority within the Christian community.

2. The Just War
22)   In the Constantinian era, as Christianity emerged from its status as an illicit underground sect to become the religion of the emperor, it found itself ready to accept the use of political and military power. Thus ended the early dominance of pacifism in the church's history. As the accepted religion of the state, Christianity now assumed obligations to the existing order. When the peace and stability of the Roman Empire were threatened by the invasion of barbarians from the north, Christians began to argue that even though war is evil, it may be justified under certain specified conditions. They called this new position the doctrine of "the just war."

23)   The theory was developed by Augustine, Bishop of Hippo in North Africa. Well educated in classical thought, he drew heavily on Plato, Aristotle, and especially Cicero in working out his ideas of a just war. This he did in his usual systematic way, as the barbarians streamed through the Alpine passes to storm and plunder Rome itself. Although another mentality, that of the Crusades, took over in the church during the later Middle Ages, the just war theory continued to attract Christian

19

thinkers. It was developed and refined by Thomas Aquinas and Francisco di Vittoria in the medieval period, the Jesuit Francisco Suares in the Reformation era, Protestant Hugo Grotius in the seventeenth century, and more recent Christian ethicists.

24)   The doctrine requires that any given war meet certain specific criteria in order to be considered just. While various thinkers since Augustine have phrased these standards differently and even varied the number, contemporary advocates of the just war theory commonly insist on these six:

(1) The war must be declared by a legitimate authority.
(2) It must be carried out with a right intention; its purpose must be to promote peace.
(3) The war must be undertaken only as a last resort. It must be a last resort to resolving conflict.
(4) It must be waged on the basis of the principle of proportionality. The relationship between ends and means must be proportionate.
(5) The war must have a reasonable chance of success.
(6) It must be waged with all the moderation possible. Particular care must be taken to see that civilian noncombatants and prisoners of war are not tortured or killed.[3]

25)   Although it attempts to sustain peace and justice by rigorously limiting armed conflict, the theory does not proscribe war, and many Christians on both sides used it to justify both World Wars. Yet despite such limitations, the theory affirms the obligation of the church and of individual Christians to form a *moral* judgment regarding any particular war, even a war duly declared by the civil power. Along with pacifism, which repudiates all participation in war, the just war theory calls for conscientious objection—not to every war, but to any war which fails to qualify under all six standards. American Christians used the just war theory to oppose the nation's waging of the War with Mexico (1846-1848) and the recent Vietnam War. In doing so, they affirmed that supreme sovereignty belongs to God rather than to the state.

3. The Crusade
26)   A third position which emerged in the Middle Ages was the idea of a crusade fought to defend Christendom against the infidel. This notion of a war for the cross has some affinity with the "holy war" of the Old Testament, but in Christian history it

did not take on major importance until the end of the eleventh century after the holy places around Jersusalem had been captured by the Turks. "Quickly the crusade was turned upon the Islamic Turkish infidels. To wage war upon non-Christians was seen as a righteous endeavor." It called for the "unquestioning participation of the Christian on the assumption that God's will was being served."[4] A common slogan was "God wills it!"

27)   Such a notion arises most naturally in a mind which assumes that its own people, civilization, and religion—despite a few understandable shortcomings—constitute the supreme expression of the divine will in history and enjoy the unique favor of God. The enemy, on the other hand, is seen as the embodiment of all that is evil and threatening to the divinely approved way of life. The mentality of the crusader is parochial, untroubled by notions of relativism or ambiguity. It carries over into the relationships between nations the ancient imagery of the religion of the Manichees: a warfare between Light and Darkness. With such a mindset the medieval crusaders readily violated the code of the just war and frequently engaged in acts of barbarism. In a "holy war" the belief "that the enemy is already damned is not conducive to chivalry."[5]

28)   It is always a temptation to see our rivals as enemies, not only of ourselves but of God, and their political system as an evil empire which we and the angels must oppose. Governments try to turn every war into a crusade. Some responsible historians have interpreted the contemporary East-West tensions as merely the latest episode in the conflict between two contrasting civilizations which goes back to the Crusades and even farther—back to the ancient wars between the Greeks and the Persians. An archaic mentality thus continues to confuse our thinking in international affairs. The justification for the Crusades, as for many other wars both before and since, relied on a questionable premise: This war is fought for the sake of peace. In such a conflict nations readily take up the language and symbols of religion. They picture their soldiers as knights in shining armor, advancing against a demonic foe in the spirit of those medieval times when "a war was conducted under the auspices of the Church for a holy cause."[6] But now the nation itself has become the object of that supreme loyalty which belongs only to God. Thus the crusading mentality falls into idolatry.

21

4. Summary

29)   Each of the basic theories or positions regarding war assumes that it insures peace, or brings peace, or keeps the peace. And each position is justified by a rationale believed to be basically Christian. Each position or attitude has been held by the church at one time or another in its history. A crucial question for us is how well do these theories or attitudes accord with the revelation of God in Jesus Christ? A similar question for our study is whether the justification used for wars in the pre-nuclear past still holds for nuclear war. Can the classical theories be applied to our new situation or has our technology rendered them obsolete?

B. The Witness of Disciples of Christ

30)   Within the larger history of world Christianity, the Christian Church (Disciples of Christ) has lived out its calling as a particular religious movement. The founders sought the unity of all Christians in freedom, believing that this sublime goal could be achieved by restoring the original church as described in the New Testament. In these troubled times to-day's Disciples seek to bear faithful witness to the gospel. From our own specific tradition we derive a measure of self-understandng and a way of approaching problems which can be briefly described.

1. A Christian Vision
of Freedom, Justice, and Peace.

31)   From the beginning Disciples of Christ have cherished the biblical dream of a world of freedom, justice, and peace. The early leaders of the movement preached the unity of the church as a condition of the conversion of the world, which would open the way for the reign of Christ. Alexander Campbell, Walter Scott, and others persistently proclaimed the Millennium. Believing in God as Creator, taking seriously the witness of the prophets, and praying "Thy Kingdom come," Disciples have expressed a vigorous concern for social problems and moral questions. This concern has been demonstrated at three levels.

32)   First, regardless of theological hue, Disciples have advocated consistency between commitment to Jesus Christ and

personal behavior. Sermons, Sunday school lessons, youth study materials, and editorial comment over the years indicate a strong concern for personal morality. At the same time there has been a wide range of accepted personal lifestyles. This latitude on such questions as tobacco, alcohol, or divorce and remarriage still exists in varying degrees across the communion. No single moral code or body of teaching has emerged as authoritative, for Disciples have always exercised personal freedom in the realm of human opinion. Although the customs of social class or region of the country have influenced the outlook of Disciples on matters of personal morality, the variation in viewpoint and practice has in no way diminished the common concern for individual integrity.

33)   Second, Disciples have responded to the biblical injunctions to care for the widow and orphan. Over the years we have joined together through various agencies and institutions to provide for those in need. We have maintained ministries with the rural and urban poor, the educationally deprived, and racial/ethnic minorities. Along with our Protestant and Roman Catholic counterparts, Disciples have provided direct services to needy persons, contributing thus to the well-being of society. This concern has grown to include the aging, exceptional persons, abused or neglected children, and refugees.

34)   Third, Disciples have been concerned with issues of public policy as these affect the general welfare of society. Alexander Campbell participated actively in the political process, serving as delegate from Brooke County to the Virginia Constitutional Convention of 1829. Three Disciples have held the office of President of the United States (James A. Garfield, Lyndon Baines Johnson, and Ronald Reagan). Senator J. William Fulbright, a Disciple from Arkansas, prodded the United States Congress to take the initiative in efforts to build peaceful relations around the world. Along with others, we have undertaken to raise consciousness, form public opinion, and influence legislation regarding particular social problems, even as many of our members have suffered from the inequities of our society. Disciples have campaigned for public schools, against Sunday closing laws ("the Lord's Day is not the Sabbath," "the mails must go through"), against (and for!) slavery, for prohibition of the liquor traffic, for civil rights, to mention some of the issues. A shelfful of resolutions passed in conven-

tions and general assemblies attests to a concern for public questions decade after decade.

35)   No moral issue has more persistently claimed the attention of Disciples than the problem of war and the concern for peace. Giving voice to the considerable popular revulsion aroused by the War with Mexico, Alexander Campbell delivered a notable oration against war.[7] During the Civil War a few influential ministers espoused pacifism on a biblical basis, but Disciples generally enlisted in the armies and supported their soldiers, their allegiance determined in nearly every case by the section of the country in which they lived.

36)   In World War I Disciples rallied to the Allied cause with nearly unanimous devotion, although the most celebrated conscientious objector, Harold Gray, came from one of our congregations. Distinguished editors and social evangelists among us (such as Charles Clayton Morrison and Harold E. Fey) led the peace movement in the postwar years and the Disciples Peace Fellowship, organized in 1935, still continues. A small but vocal minority in the past half century has taken a firm pacifist stand. At the same time, some of the best known generals in World War II and subsequent conflicts (such as General Omar Bradley, General Maxwell Taylor) have been Disciples.

37)   Through the years the International Convention of Disciples of Christ, succeeded by the General Assembly of the Christian Church (Disciples of Christ), has approved a long series of resolutions on peace among nations. In 1921 the convention sent a telegram to President Harding in support of the Conference on Disarmament, hailing it as a step "in preventing war, relieving the people of unbearable burden of taxation and setting free the world's resources" for constructive social purposes. The recent World War had demonstrated that "preparation begets, not stifles war." Support for disarmament recurs in resolutions of subsequent assemblies, along with general opposition to war, advocacy of conciliation and arbitration in international disputes, and affirmations of interdependence in a global community. After World War II the convention urged a relaxation of the tensions between the U.S.A. and the U.S.S.R., affirming, "Nations with radically different political economies can live together in peace and amity if there is the will to

do so." That 1946 convention also called for international control of atomic energy with safeguards against its use in war. Since that time Disciples have continued to call on the great powers to agree on a plan for dismantling their nuclear arsenals.

38)   As to military service, Disciples acknowledge both the citizen's duty to support the state and the right of individual conscience in refusal to bear arms. Resolutions have repeatedly opposed peacetime conscription and military training programs in high schools and colleges, but in 1971 the General Assembly defeated a proposal to declare the Christian Church (Disciples of Christ) a "peace church" with a witness similar to that of the Friends, the Brethren, and the Mennonites. Churches have been urged to hold in fellowship both those who accept military service and those who refuse it on grounds of conscience. Support has also been registered for selective conscientious objection based on the criteria for a "just war."

39)   It is evident then that despite a common concern for the well-being of society, all Disciples have rarely taken the same position on any particular social issue. In the days of slavery, for example, most black Disciples were held in bondage. Some white Disciples opposed the system, some defended it, some urged that it was a matter of politics and economics and consequently of indifference for Christians. In general, it was Southern white Disciples who upheld it, black Disciples along with Northern and Canadian white Disciples who resisted it, and white Disciples in the border states who wanted the church to keep silent or who took a pacifist stand during the Civil War. Not until two or three generations had passed did Disciples generally attain sufficient emotional detachment to recognize the profound effect of sectional attitudes on religious convictions in that tragic era.

40)   Such disagreement makes it clear that even Christians who take the scriptures seriously may nevertheless reach radically different conclusions on a matter of public policy. Our social thinking as Christians is conditioned, often unconsciously, by our particular time and place, by the culture of which we are a part. This process will undoubtedly affect our efforts as Disciples to determine our stance regarding nuclear weapons. Recognition of the influence of culture should not deter us in

the quest for an understanding that transcends and transforms culture.

2. Approaches to Social Concerns

41)   On the basis of Disciples' historic commitment to freedom, justice, and peace, can a characteristic approach to public issues be established? Although we have formulated no authoritative body of teaching on personal morality or social ethics (or theology or anything else), we Disciples have tended to do our thinking in a particular way. We have much more in common in this familiar way of dealing with an issue than in the specific positions to which such thinking may lead us.

42)   At the outset Disciples professed to speak where the Scriptures speak, to base our positions on the Bible alone. Yet as we have approached the Bible on matters of belief and ethics, the values of reasonableness and of freedom have profoundly affected the way in which we have read it and consequently what we have found. Disciples insist on the right to make up our own minds in the light of our best understanding of the biblical message concerning Jesus Christ.

43)   Disciples regard the Scriptures as witness to God's self-revelation in the history of Israel and in the ministry of Jesus. Since this sacred literature grows out of responses in faith across a span of more than a thousand years, we have insisted on sound historical and literary methods in studying it. Study of this kind requires the effort to understand accurately the original setting, intent, and meaning of a passage as well as to undertake appropriate applications to life today. Disciples have followed Alexander Campbell and earlier scholars of the Reformed tradition in distinguishing among the various covenants set forth in scripture (God's covenants with Noah, Abraham, Moses, David, and finally the new covenant in Jesus Christ). We have held that Jewish law is not binding on the church and that many early passages reflect notions about God which Jesus explicitly repudiated. In his "Address on War" Alexander Campbell specifically denied that the martial exploits of Old Testament heroes are models for Christians.

44)   In matters about which the Scriptures are silent Disciples have followed Campbell in taking a pragmatic approach to a problem. In the absence of a "thus saith the Lord," he com-

mended the "law of expediency"—the principle of adopting the best discernible present means of attaining any given end, or "of adopting the most promising means for the discovery of what our aims should be."[8] Whether an insight comes directly from a biblical text or from prudential wisdom, Disciples have sought to weigh every thought against the mind of Christ.

45)   Disciples have commended a reasonable approach to all matters of religion. We place high value on the use of the mind in searching out the meaning of scripture and its appropriateness for guidance in any given circumstance. This concern for plain common sense has led us to disdain emotionalism and mystical claims to knowledge on the one hand and dogmatic rationalism on the other, with its insistence on an orthodoxy to which all thought and action must conform. The Disciples' commitment to reasonableness includes a concern to search out all available essential information in the process of making a theological or ethical decision. We have esteemed learning and research, with openness to the natural and social sciences. Not without conflict and differences of opinion, we have modified earlier positions in light of new evidence. This approach may be described as empirical and inductive.

46)   A key characteristic of Disciples in our approach to any social issue is the high value we place on freedom. From our early nineteenth-century origins to the present, we have championed the rights of individuals, congregations, and groups of Christians to reach and hold their own convictions. Considering freedom a right grounded in the dignity which God bestows on every human being, we have specifically guaranteed it in *The Design for the Christian Church (Disciples of Christ)*. It would be far too much to claim that Disciples have never fallen into intolerance. But the movement has explicitly and repeatedly appealed to freedom as a norm by which its common life could be measured and its failures judged. The wide variety of points of view on any social issue manifests the common regard for freedom of inquiry and freedom of thought: "in essentials unity, in opinions liberty." The Panel's preparation of this message on peace and the various responses to it both give expression to that freedom which Disciples have valued so highly as an affirmation of personal and corporate integrity.

47)   Disciples have sought to approach social problems in

27

consultation with other people of good will. The founders of the Disciples movement insisted that they were not advancing a peculiar interpretation of scripture, but were following the generally accepted understanding of the meaning of biblical words. In dealing with questions of supreme importance they appealed to the "common mind" of the Christian world. Thus in struggling with difficult points of church doctrine and practice Disciples have undertaken to work within an ecumenical context. We have been influenced in our approach to social questions by prevailing trends of thought and action within the larger Christian community and, as already noted, by prevalent trends in the wider social setting. In the preparation of this document the panel has carefully considered *A Pastoral Letter on War and Peace* issued by the National Conference of Catholic Bishops as well as studies by numerous other denominational and ecumenical bodies.

3. Summary

48)   Disciples of Christ variously subscribe to a wide range of opinion on matters of social concern as a consequence of several factors, including our approach to the issues (scriptural, reasonable, empirical, inductive, freedom-loving, ecumenical) and the human propensity for reflecting the perspectives and values of our own social context. Yet throughout this diversity run high expectations for Christian discipleship: the worth of persons, an integrity linking belief with behavior, a commitment to responsible participation in the common life, and a powerful hope, springing from our Christian faith, for the future of the human enterprise. But now the nuclear reality confronts Disciples, along with all people everywhere, with a new and overwhelming problem.

II. From Personal Combat to Nuclear Warfare

49)   While the Christian conscience has struggled for centuries with the evils of waging war, the nature and scope of the military enterprise have been transformed. A review of the evolution in our ability to kill one another shows a steady increase in lethal power. The technological advance which multiplies the destructive force of armaments has brought two other significant effects. 1) It increased the distance of the combatants from one another so that the fighter who discharges a weapon may never see the impact of the shell or bomb, while the victims it strikes have no personal encounter whatever with their assailant. 2) It intertwined the production of arms and military supplies more deeply with the economic and intellectual processes of society.

50)   As a result, responding ethically to the issues of war becomes incredibly complex, even as it becomes more essential to human survival. The ethical thinking of the past dealt with situations far simpler than our own. It is important therefore to note the radical changes in the mode and scale of warfare and to take account of the unprecedented threat to human survival posed by the reality of nuclear weapons.

A. The Expansion of Military Power

51)   War was first waged by antagonists fighting hand to hand, one against the other. With the development of clubs, then swords, then spears, the antagonists drew farther apart while increasing their ability to wound and kill. Bows and arrows, and then long-bows, increased the distance, and with the invention of powder and guns, the distances grew still greater.

Guns evolved into cannons, increasing both the range of the projectiles and the number of persons who might be injured with a single shot. It became possible to kill enemies without seeing them. In 1944-45 guided missiles and saturation bombing further multiplied both distance and destructiveness, as did the unleashing of the first atomic bombs. It was only a short step to ICBMs armed with nuclear explosives and another to satellite systems designed to rain destruction from outer space. The attraction of militarism is closely intertwined with the development of the nation-state and is systematically linked with forces for good as well as forces for evil. This involvement underlies the ambiguity and intransigence of military power.

1. The Military-Commercial Complex
52)   The commercialization of war, or the "Military-Commercial Complex," emerged during the fourteenth century when small professional armies of mercenary soldiers were employed by the Italian city-states to protect the economic interests of the traders. As a consequence the commercial economy prospered and the city-states found surpluses in their treasuries coming from taxation of the new commercial wealth. The city-states used the taxes to underwrite the cost of their armies, which became powerful instruments of policy in the hands of the magistrates, the political leaders.

53)   Living under a government with such a military instrument at its disposal was an advantage for the commercial interests because of the protection it provided for their enterprise. For the magistrates it was an advantage to permit the tradesmen of the marketplace to pursue unlimited profit wherever they desired because it brought dramatic growth in tax receipts to help maintain the standing armies as instruments integral to their pursuit of power.

2. The Military-Industrial Complex
54)   The industrialization of war, or the "Military-Industrial Complex," dates from the 1840s with the introduction of semi-automated mass production, steam power, and railroads. The keys to unlocking the industrial revolution were interchangeable parts and improved means of transportation. Mass production, in turn, allowed the standardization of military equipment which could be produced at much lower costs. Instead of small professional armies numbered in thousands,

soldiers could now be conscripted from the citizenry, counted in millions, and transported and supplied nearly anywhere on the globe. Armies were composed of obedient, replaceable parts. War became industrialized and industry found it profitable to become militarized, a circumstance which permitted war to occur on a world scale in the twentieth century with international interchange of weapons and personnel.

3. The Military-Technological Complex

55)   Our new era, the "Military-Technological Complex," is witness to a major emphasis upon new weapons research. Believing that advances in the development of directed energy devices such as lasers and particle beam weapons hold the promise of an impenetrable defense against nuclear attack, some U.S. leaders are vigorously promoting a new multi-billion-dollar Strategic Defense Initiative (SDI), popularly referred to as Star Wars. There is widespread skepticism in the scientific community about the viability of such a program. Yet with the full support of the political authorities (the magistrates), the research of scientists and technicians continues unabated. Armaments have become so lethal, and military services employing them so specialized and so set apart from the civilian population, that mass armies as we have known them will likely become obsolete.

56)   Along with increased distances and destructiveness, modern warfare involves entire populations in national efforts of building armaments. The proliferation of nuclear weapons and delivery systems exacts an astronomical cost, diverting a heavy flow of human and financial resources from areas of desperate human need. Every minute the world's military budget absorbs $1.3 million of public funds, and every minute thirty children die for want of food and vaccines. The cost of a single new nuclear submarine equals the annual budgets for education of 23 developing countries with 160,000,000 school-age children. During 1982-83 the government of the U.S.A. spent twice as much on military research as on civilian research.

57)   The pressure to devise ever more sophisticated weaponry usurps the capabilities of our best research facilities and robs other areas of our common life of the genius of our best minds. Popular fears of foreign attack, exacerbated by the

arms race and exploited for political advantage, turn the will of the people from humanitarian causes to a mood of defensiveness and even aggression. Deterrent strategies feed on insecurity, and proponents of greater military expenditures commonly cultivate distrust of other nations. The demands of the military-technological complex distort our stewardship of the resources God has given. The long and successful partnership of the magistrates and the military and the marketplace continues to produce highly sophisticated armaments for the defense of their mutual interests and the protection of society at large. But by an awful irony the ultimate weapon of defense has also become the threat of ultimate destruction.[9]

B. The Nuclear Age

58)   At 8:10 a.m. on August 6, 1945, the city of Hiroshima became the first target for the military use of nuclear power. That Japanese city of 340,000 was all but obliterated. Sixty-eight percent of its buildings were totally destroyed or made unusable. Seventy thousand of its citizens were killed. Even after forty years, the full impact of that bomb is still not fully known. Long-term radiation sickness, other physical and psychological consequences of the blast, and the genetic effects continue to be studied and evaluated. There is much that we do not know—but one thing is clear: A new and terrible age had dawned in the history of humanity.

1. A Relentless Technology

59)   The intervening years have witnessed the relentless spread of nuclear technology. This occurred for a while under the theme of "atoms for peace" when peacetime applications for the generation of electrical power were believed to offer a permanent and inexpensive solution to the energy needs of the world. It also occurred as several advanced nations sought to acquire the capability of military application of nuclear power. Today, there are two nuclear superpowers: the U.S.A. and the U.S.S.R. In addition, several other nations are known to have nuclear weapons and the means for their delivery, while several more nations are known to have the capability of producing such weapons, whether or not they have actually done so.

60)   Because national security demands military secrecy, the general public does not have full and verifiable data con-

cerning the present collective military application of nuclear power. A conservative estimate indicates that most of the nuclear warheads today are much more powerful than the bomb that was used at Hiroshima—at least fifty times and probably eighty times as powerful! The destructive power of the global nuclear arsenal is 5,000 times greater than that of all the munitions used in World War II. It is also well known that all of the major metropolitan centers of the Soviet Union, Western Europe and North America are already pre-targeted.

61)   Against nuclear weapons there is *no* known, reliable defense. For forty years, the world has witnessed the amassing of this destructive power without being able to curtail its growth. U.S. foreign policy has been based largely on the assumption that only the reality of Mutual Assured Destruction (MAD) had thus far prevented the use of the nuclear weapons. However, in recent years both the U.S.S.R. and the U.S.A. have shifted their policies toward a new stance which assumes the probability of nuclear war and seeks to achieve survival. The new U.S.A. policy called Nuclear Utilization Target Selection (NUTS) seems even more ominous than the earlier one. Thus an entire generation of women and men have lived under an incessant threat of annihilation.

2. Effects of Nuclear War
62)   In recent years, scientists have moved toward a comprehensive understanding of the total effects of a nuclear war. Exhaustive studies of the actual military use of the bombs at Hiroshima and Nagasaki, and of the many experimental explosions have begun to fill in the picture. The general public has come to perceive these effects through the reading of many books and articles, and the viewing of numerous films which graphically depict the impact of nuclear war.

63)   Reliable studies have been published which describe the effects of the initial blast of a one-megaton bomb, the factors which will determine the extent of the radioactive fallout and the duration of its effects, the awesome power of the thermal radiation, and the magnitude of the incineration of people and properties which would result from a nuclear blast, the electromagnetic pulse which would disrupt all electric systems over vast areas, and the almost total disruption of the organized, institutional life of a modern society. All of these

dimensions of nuclear war have been rather thoroughly researched and evaluated.

64)   But the more enduring and elusive effects of nuclear war continue to be areas about which there is only limited knowledge. These areas seem to be two in number: the impact on the ecology and the long-term effects on the genetic heritage of the human race. As awesome as are the known risks, the unknown factors are even more terrifying. The Office of Technical Assessment of the Congress of the United States affirms that the effects of a nuclear war that cannot be calculated are at least as important as those for which calculations are attempted. Nobody knows how to estimate the likelihood that industrial civilization might collapse in the areas attacked or to judge the probability of long-term ecological damage.[10]

65)   Our dilemma is not just that we do not know the possible disastrous effects of a total nuclear war, but that we can never know! As Jonathan Schell cogently reasons in *The Fate of the Earth*, we are only permitted to speculate on the genetic and ecological effects, since the actual unleashing of a total nuclear war would, in all likelihood, so devastate the earth as to make human life as we know it improbable. We cannot "experiment" with the destruction of the ozone layer without running the risk of the extinction of the human species!

66)   One might summarize the present state of understanding of the effects of a nuclear war as follows: (a) the effects upon individual lives can be more or less predicted; (b) the effects on human society can be only generally predicted; (c) the effects on subsequent generations can be projected only in a very general way and almost without verifiable data; and finally, (d) the effects on the natural environment are almost totally speculation.

3. A New Situation
67)   The crucial question posed for us in the nuclear age is this: Is nuclear warfare substantively different from conventional warfare, and if so, in what ways? There are certain dimensions of the nuclear reality which basically represent a *difference in degree* in comparison with the problems posed by earlier forms of warfare.

68)   Illustrative of these "degree differences" are the following aspects of modern warfare:

- the sheer increase of destructive power. It could be argued that the release of energy from the atom represented simply another stage in the utilization of power already used in earlier and more limited forms for the waging of war.
- the growing impersonal nature of warfare. The detonation of a nuclear device can be seen as only the latest stage of what has been a historic trend away from face-to-face combat and toward a more remote and impersonal means of destruction.
- the question of responsible governmental or civilian control of the armed forces. Modern democracies have aspired to keep the control of military forces clearly in the hands of a civilian government, but as technology has advanced and the time-span for decision-making has been shortened, this control has been eroded. Nuclear warfare can be seen as simply the latest stage of this growing and crucial issue.

69)   Thus we see that nuclear warfare represents a new degree or a new stage in a development which has historical precedents. However, it can be argued that the degree of change in the nuclear age is of such magnitude that traditional ways of making moral judgments on warfare are no longer applicable.

4. Unprecedented Moral Issues

70)   Beyond the differences of degree, moreover, other substantive dimensions of nuclear warfare raise *moral questions* beyond any that were ever raised by conventional weapons. Illustrative of these questions are the following:

71)   (1) *The possibility of human extinction.* Heretofore, war posed a threat to individual lives; and in some cases, such as genocide, a threat to entire groups, tribes or classes of people. Nuclear warfare poses the possibility of the extinction of the entire human race—the total destruction of humanity. No human generation has ever faced this awesome possibility before.

72)   (2) *The possibility of the destruction of a life-sustaining natural environment.* War in the past has devastated large areas of the surface of the earth. However, the possibility of the destruction of the ozone layer by an all-out nuclear war poses the prospect of the elimination of a life-sustaining environment

35

except for certain minimal forms of life such as "insects and grass,"[11] the onset of a "nuclear winter" rendering this planet devoid of life as we know it.

73) (3) *The weakening or distorting of the genetic heritage of the race.* It has been demonstrated beyond any reasonable doubt that radioactive fallout can have far-reaching effects on human genes. An all-out nuclear war involves the possibility not just of killing the present generation in large numbers, but of working fundamental changes in the genetic "treasure" of the entire human race. Such a possibility poses the awesome question of the right of any generation to corrupt or degrade all future unborn generations. If we are admonished in scripture "not [to] fear those who kill the body" but rather the one "who can destroy both soul and body in hell" (Mt.10:28), it could be validly asked whether or not the possibility of a "hell of deformed and degraded beings" does not pose for us a different question than the one posed by conventional warfare which "killed the body."

74) (4) *The practical elimination of defensive possibilities.* Most moral systems in the past have made some distinction between the use of violence for conquest and attack, on the one hand, and the possession of instruments of defense (shields, moats, etc.) on the other. In the nuclear age all weaponry is for offense, not actually a means of defense. There are no reliable means of defense. Thus the nuclear age has placed humanity in a new ethical situation, a situation further complicated by the arguments of some policy-makers that only a "first strike" offers any hope of partial survival for a nation. Does this mean that technology has placed us in a position in which survival is possible only by the abandonment of our highest moral teachings about offensive war?

75) (5) *The unpredictability of a total nuclear war.* Conventional warfare has been experienced and studied sufficiently that it is possible to make reasonable predictions about its consequences. Since ethical decision-making always calls for an evaluation of the effects of an action, some ethicists have proposed a moral justification for war along the lines of the "end justifying the means." However, the nuclear age now confronts us with the possibility of destruction beyond our ability to imagine, measure, or describe. The best authorities affirm

36

that what we "do not know" is as important as, or more important than, what we "do know." In light of the unknowability of the effects of nuclear war on the genetic heritage of the race and the natural environment, are we not faced with a situation in which basic morality as we have traditionally understood it, makes it impossible to advocate, endorse or participate in nuclear war?

76)   The nuclear age is only forty years old. We confess to a limited understanding of all that it means and the issues which it poses. One thing, however, is clear to us: The nuclear age poses new questions and issues which cannot be addressed by traditional assumptions about warfare and patriotism. Since history cannot be reversed and armed conflict between major powers now holds the possibility of becoming a nuclear war, we are called to search for new ethical insights and principles which relate creatively and directly to the issues posed for today's humanity grimly hoping to survive the nuclear age.

III. Christian Resources for Peacemaking

77)   It is now time for us to work through our heritage as Christians in a search for those resources which may help us in making peace. We explore the witness of scripture, certain basic themes in Christian thought, and some essential considerations in Christian ethics. We shall then move to our final chapter with some practical conclusions on peacemaking in the nuclear age.

78)   How then shall we respond to the strange new terror of nuclear arms—we who are called to be peacemakers? We are clearly not satisfied with the arms race as it is. It is one thing for us to make up our own minds about what should be done to depart from the present evil and do good. It is another to find a way to influence the decision-makers in magistracy, military, and marketplace in this and other nations, so that they will do the same.

A. *The Biblical Vision of Peace* (Shalom)

79)   As Christians we intentionally turn to the Bible for guidance. One of the key themes in scripture is peace, perhaps best represented by the Hebrew word *shalom*. It is depicted in the stories of people in ancient Israel who were led to understand that God was with them, and it comes to climax in the life and ministry of Jesus and the rise of the church.

80)   In opening our minds and hearts to the message of the Bible we enter a realm of profound spiritual insight and energizing power. Christians generally affirm the inspiration of the Bible. The phrase carries a double meaning. (1) God inspired

39

the Scriptures. The Holy Spirit moved women and men of ancient times to speak and write concerning what God had done among them. (2) The Scriptures inspire the faithful. Those who reverently read and diligently study these Scriptures are thus brought into contact with the living God. In doing so we are confronted with the demands of God, the judgment of God, the love and grace of God. Regular and continuing engagement with the sacred text opens our understanding to the mind of Christ, and we find what it means to live by faith.

81)   The affirmation about the inspiration of the Holy Scriptures stands in creative tension with literary and historical methods of Bible study. We are dealing with a collection of varied literature, diverse in its understandings, coming out of the experience of hundreds of people, across a long period of time. Each passage reflects the understanding of a particular writer. It is limited by that writer's own mental outlook, personal circumstances, and intention in addressing a specific audience. At the same time, it is inspired and speaks out of an intense awareness of the reality of God and with heightened insight resulting from that encounter. (Recall that paragraphs 41-48 deal with this tension in Disciples tradition.)

82)   The problems of the nuclear age ought not be approached by prooftexting—lifting an isolated passage or two out of context to put the stamp of divine authority on an idea we want to advance. So great is the danger of such a procedure that Alexander Campbell once counseled against preaching a sermon based on any single text. Disciples tend to say, "Job says . . . , Paul says . . . , Jesus says . . . ," rather than "The Bible says. . . ." When we quote a text, we do so because it aptly summarizes a pervasive biblical motif. This method is quite different from the legalism and triumphalism that motivates the use of prooftexts.

83)   Much of the Bible was written in times of violent wars, merciless destruction, and exultation over calamities befalling enemies. Many passages breathe with the heat of battle, calling on God's aid in bringing down the foe. The book accurately reflects the spirit of that era. Many of its noblest characters are warriors, and God deals graciously with this company of military heroes.

84)   Even so, the Bible overall does not advocate military preparedness or war. Quite the contrary, even in its most war-like passages the same prophets who invoked death and destruction on Israel's enemies resisted the people in their lust for a powerful king to make them like other nations; they rebuked the kings for building up the armed forces and for establishing foreign alliances. These early prophets believed that God would fight Israel's battles and deliver them from their foes. They reminded Israel that it was the Lord who brought them out of Egyptian slavery, not their own might (1 S 8:4-20). The stories of Gideon, Elijah, and Elisha make clear that deliverance comes from God (Jg 7:2-9, 2 K 1, 7). Jeremiah counseled so vigorously against military action even in wartime as to provoke his arrest for treason (Jr 38:1-6). The prophets clung stubbornly to the faith that the Lord of history would work out their deliverance, using as instruments of the divine purpose those unwitting nations whose clashing ambitions seemed to threaten Israel's very existence. (Is 10:5-11; Jr 27:1-7). No major prophet advocated what nationalists would view as a "responsible" foreign policy. Vengeance was to be left to God (Pr 25:21-22; Rm 12:20). The Bible is not a directive for military policy, nor a handbook of diplomacy, nor a manual for the conduct of war.

85)   So we address ourselves to one of the major themes of scripture. Each aspect of *shalom* will require extended study. But here we suggest the heart of the matter, the application of *shalom* insights to our own dilemma about nuclear war and the superpowers' arms race. This study is not just an intellectual exercise, nor an occasion to justify our own inclinations. It is a venture in faith which calls us to committed obedience and action.

1. *Shalom* as God's Promise

86)   The great biblical vision of oneness, of wholeness, is the vision of God's *shalom*. It cannot be reduced to a simple definition or formula, for *shalom* is a vision. Used throughout the Hebrew scriptures, the word includes many concepts, such as wholeness, peace, healing, justice, righteousness, salvation, freedom, oneness, prosperity, and well-being.

87)   This biblical *shalom* is an enduring vision of God's promise to all creation. It is the promise that swords can be

turned into plowshares (Is 2:4; Mi 4:3), the promise that the wolf shall dwell with the lamb (Is 11:6-9), the promise of peace in the land (Lv 26:4-6; Zc 9:9-12), and the promise of justice for all (Dt 15:1-11; Is 1:1-9; Ps 72).

88)   God's promise is an enduring vision of hope (Jr 29:10-14), expressed in times much like our own when it is very difficult to embrace hope (Is 65:21). Isaiah made the promise to a people in exile. *Shalom* affirms that God wills a future. God holds out hope even to those in captivity (Jr 29).

89)   For Christians, Jesus Christ became the embodiment of *shalom*. He lived out God's vision in human history reconciling the world to God (2 Co 5:19; Jn 3:16). Jesus became our peace (Ep 2:14), and we are the heirs of that vision according to God's promise (Ga 3:28-29). Jesus came to preach peace, to manifest it by his life and love, and to bring us together so that there might be wholeness, unity, and peace in the family of God (Ep 2:17-22). He came to fulfill the promise of *shalom*, to proclaim the acceptable year of the Lord when justice would reign for all. Jesus came proclaiming that the promise found in Isaiah was being fulfilled in preaching good news to the poor, declaring release for the captives, giving sight to the blind, and bringing liberty to the oppressed (Lk 4:16-21).

90)   Jesus' ministry to the excluded, to the broken victims of life, was spent in re-establishing God's will for *shalom*, bringing reconciliation to a fragmented world, with justice and mercy for all. In the Sermon on the Mount he boldly declared that those who seek justice and mercy, those who are peace-makers, are not only blessed but are to be known as the children of God (Mt 5:1-9).

91)   God's promise of *shalom* recurs throughout scripture, from the beginning to the end. In the beginning, God created a garden of peace with all that is needed for a good life (Gn 2:8-9), and at the end this promise is expressed most vividly in John's vision of a new Jerusalem where all things are made new (Rv 21:1-6). In the meantime, it is the continual message of the good that God promises and wills for all creation.

2. Unity of God's Creation

92)   Throughout the Bible runs a central theme: We are

created to be one. There is an intentional unity of all creation, and each of us is a member of God's family with special responsibility for the care of all that God has made. The prophetic vision saw all people drawn into community around the will of God to live in peace and harmony with one another (Is 2:2-4). The New Testament envisioned all persons drawn together as believers under the lordship of Jesus Christ (Mt 28:16-20; Jn 12:32) into a single community (Jn 10:15-16; 12:32). In Jesus Christ, we, who were once strangers to the covenants of promise, living without hope and without God in the world, are now made one with him and are reconciled to God in one body (Ep 2:11-22).

93)   These sweeping visions of the unity of God's creation constantly remind us that we are all members of one family, God's family, and are "heirs of a single hope, and bearers of a single destiny, namely, the care and management of all of God's creation."[12] This is the persistent message in the Bible expressed time and again in the life of the early church. The authors reflect often on the unity of God's people because Jesus is our peace, making us one by breaking down the dividing wall of hostility (Ep 2:12-15). There is neither Greek nor Jew, slave nor free, male nor female, for we are all one in Christ Jesus (Ga 3:28-29). All things were created through him, and all things are held together by him because in him God was reconciling to himself all things (Col. 1:3-20).

94)   Here all are members of one household (Ep 2:19), one body in Christ (Rm 12:4-5); as one body all suffer when even one member suffers (1 Co 12:12-26). The oneness confessed by Christians is a gift from God, bestowed on all people from the beginning of time, but most vividly manifested in the life and ministry of Jesus who sought to bring us all to the realization of that oneness intended by God in the act of our creation (Jn 17:20-26).

3. Justice
95)   The demand for justice is central to the biblical vision of *shalom*. God's intervention in Israel's history, especially in light of the Exodus, is seen as the recurring enactment of justice. The faithful are called to do justice because God is just. "Justice" and "righteousness" render into English the same Hebrew word; biblical ethics is concerned therefore with both

social justice and personal integrity. Liberation from oppression is grounded in God's demand for justice. The biblical concern for the poor and for human rights reflects the centrality of justice.

96)   Biblical justice points to the will of God disclosed in Israel's history and in Jesus Christ for establishing personal and social arrangements which protect, nurture, and enhance human life. Justice has to do with the restraint of evil and with vindicating the wronged. Biblical justice is more than maintenance of public order and retribution for the lawbreaker. Justice in the biblical sense also deals with the formation of new personal and societal relationships which allow for the growth of persons, the expression of human creativity, and the expansion of the common good.

97)   The prophets of Israel and Judah made justice their central theme. Faithfulness to the covenant was to be expressed in righteousness and justice:

Let justice roll down like waters,
    and righteousness like an everflowing stream.   —Am 5:24

He has showed you, O man, what is good;
    and what does the LORD require of you
but to do justice, and to love kindness,
    and to walk humbly with your God?   —Mi 6:8

To the king of Judah Jeremiah directs his word:

Thus says the LORD: Do justice and righteousness, and deliver from the hand of the oppressor him who has been robbed. And do no wrong or violence to the alien, the fatherless, and the widow, nor shed innocent blood in this place.   —Jr 22:3

Jesus began his public ministry by reading from Isaiah a passage which linked the centrality of justice in Israel with his own mission:

The Spirit of the Lord is upon me,
because he has anointed me to preach
    good news to the poor.

He has sent me to proclaim release to the captives
and recovering of sight to the blind,
to set at liberty those who are oppressed,
to proclaim the acceptable year of the Lord.   *—Lk 4:18-19*

98)   Justice is the foundation of peace. The claim of justice
is prior to that of peace in the biblical witness.[13] "Peace must be
built on the basis of justice in a world where the personal and
social consequences of sin are evident."[14] Justice and peace are
inextricably bound, for "the tree of peace has justice for its
roots."[15]

4. Peace
99)   One of the manifestations of God's *shalom* is an ideal
world in which there is no war. Indeed, *shalom* is frequently
defined as peace in the narrow sense, i.e., absence of war. While
this definition falls considerably short of capturing the full
meaning of *shalom*, it is an important and legitimate ingre-
dient of the concept. Because of the cruelty and frequency of
war in biblical times, there was a deep yearning for the day
when God's world would be so ordered that conflict would
cease and war would be no more.

100)   Both the Law (Lv 26:3-6) and the Prophets (Is 2:4; Mi
4:3) present classical expressions of this hope. While inter-
preters differ as to whether the peace pictured in these words is
meant for our time or for an idyllic time to come, the meaning
is clear and appealing:

He shall judge between the nations,
    and shall decide for many peoples;
and they shall beat their swords into plowshares,
    and their spears into pruning hooks;
nation shall not lift up sword against nation,
    neither shall they learn war any more.   *(Is 2:4)*

Isaiah adds (11:6-9):
The wolf shall dwell with the lamb,
    and the leopard shall lie down with the kid,
and the calf and the lion and the fatling together,
    and a little child shall lead them. . . .
They shall not hurt or destroy in
    all my holy mountain;

for the earth shall be full of the
knowledge of the LORD
as the waters cover the sea.

101) These descriptions of the longed-for peaceable kingdom have two clear implications: 1) No individual can enjoy
this peace in isolation from the community. Rather, peace for
the individual requires the larger setting of peace for the nation
or the community as a whole. 2) Individual peace is necessarily
part of a larger peace throughout God's ordered world. A
ravaged world cannot house a peaceful humankind.

102) When the Roman legions dominated the earth with
unprecedented military power, Jesus came among us. Scripture
depicts him as Prince of Peace, as Suffering Servant, as Lamb
led to the slaughter, as Victim returning good for evil. Yet Jesus
attracted the faith of soldiers, accepted their trust, and
ministered to their needs. He constantly embodied love and
peace, and encouraged his followers to do the same. "Blessed
are the peacemakers," he said (Mt 5:9), "for they shall be called
children of God." Thus Jesus imposes on his followers not a passive role as peacekeepers, but the active role of peacemaking.

103) Jesus' attitude toward peace must be drawn from ev-
erything that we know about his life and ministry. Some isolated statements taken out of context are likely to mislead the
casual reader. For example, in proclaiming the Reign of God
with its radical judgment on the prevailing ways of the world,
he expressed that tension in striking imagery: "I have not come
to bring peace, but a sword" (Mt 10:34; compare Lk 22:36). A
careful study of the context in which such sayings occur makes
it clear that in no way do they provide a charter for the military
enterprise; rather they use the imagery of war to indicate the
intensity of spiritual conflict, as does also the stirring passage in
Ephesians: "Put on the whole armor of God" (Ep 6:10-17).
Throughout his ministry Jesus consistently revealed that freedom, justice, and love bring about the peace of God's reign.

5. The Covenant
104) Relationship with God is an ethical relationship.
God's people are all bonded by covenant with God: God promises to be with the covenant-people and to give strength and
courage for carrying out the task to which they are called (Lk

21:12-19). The covenant binds them to obedience, pledged to live in response to the needs of others and to care for all of God's creation.

105)   God initiated a covenant with the people of Israel, a covenant of peace, promising security in the land, showers of blessing in season, and deliverance from slavery, hunger, and suffering (Ezk 34:25-29). The theme carries over in letters to the early church: God has likewise initiated a covenant with those who are called in Christ to be also the offspring of Abraham and heirs according to the promise (Ga 3:29). It is a covenant made with God's people for a time of full empowerment, acceptance, and belonging. It is a promise by God who is ever faithful to God's people (Rm 8:19-39).

106)   The covenant-call to be God's people, far from being primarily an invitation to special privilege, is first of all a summons to special responsibility. God calls a people to live in response to the needs of others, to live in right relationship with God, to bring justice and mercy to the land, and to lead the way toward peace and freedom. The covenant binds Israel to trust in God alone, not putting confidence in false prophets or false securities (Ezk 13:16; Jr 6:14; 8:10-12; Is 7:1-9; 30:1-4).

107)   We who accept the covenant are called to be ministers of reconciliation and to make God's peace visible through the love and the unity within our own communities (2 Co 5:18-21). The commandment given to love our enemies (Mt 5:39-45) and to pray for those who persecute us, even to bless those who persecute us, and to feed our enemies if they are hungry, or give them drink if they are thirsty, is vital to this ministry of reconciliation (Rm 12:14-21). We are to love one another as Jesus loved his disciples (Jn 15:12-17).

108)   Being faithful to this covenant is not an easy task, for *shalom* has not yet been fully realized. But we have the promise that God wills to establish an everlasting covenant of peace, and we have God's promise to be with us forever (Jr 31:31-34; Ezk 37:26). Jesus' last words, according to the writer of the first gospel, were a sending forth and a promise to be always with those who keep faith with the covenant-mission (Mt 28:16-20). Our faithfulness requires intentionality, patience, and commitment.

109)   How can we live toward God's vision of *shalom*? Can we embrace it, make it our own, and begin living toward the realization of God's vision of unity, peace, and justice? In this time of great fear, hostility, and brokenness, can we trust in *shalom* as God's promise? Does this promise affect the way we live and feel? Assuming we are all created to be one, what does God's purpose in creation say to us about our enemies? If we are all members of one family, how can we engage in preparation for possible total destruction of others, and ourselves as well? In what ways does the covenant-call to be God's people lay on us a special task or responsibility for peacemaking?

B. Some Basic Themes in Christian Faith

110)   As we open our lives to the witness of scripture, we find ourselves confronted, like the men and women we meet in its pages, by the inescapable reality of the eternal God. This confrontation impels us to worship, to serve, and to ponder the mysteries of our human condition in encounter with the divine. Theology is the name for this reasoning about God, and "doing theology" is a work of faith which necessarily involves us in a dialogue between scripture and our own situation.

111)   In our theologizing we cannot forget that we live in the nuclear age. Rather our calling as Christians compels us to think anew concerning the meaning of convictions long held by the church. We focus briefly on four topics of special importance for all who are engaged with the issues of nuclear warfare.

1. The Living God
112)   The God of Scripture is involved in the world. In the thick of our personal and public struggles this God meets us with the calling to share in the divine work of forming creation in justice. God is not removed or detached from worldly involvements; the loving God of creation is also the purposeful God of history: "I am the LORD your God, who brought you out of the land of Egypt, out of the house of bondage" (Ex 20:2). In this world of perplexity and fear, God is actively present.

113)   The living God of creation is a God of compassion and of wrath. This God is moved by compassion to agony over hu-

48

man suffering, and by wrath to indignation at the heedlessness of the privileged and the powerful, who enjoy the perquisites of wealth and position with no concern for the downtrodden. This divine wrath is directed not only at deliberate exploiters, but even at comfortable and complacent worshipers who are indifferent to the suffering and plight of others (Am 2:6-8; 5:21-24; Mt 23:2-5, 23).

114)   One of the most profound advances in "the progress of revealed light"[16] came through the prophets in this disclosure of God's wrath, even against those most earnestly engaged in religious worship and obedience. This revelation was a revolution in biblical thought. When the people of Israel had been nobody, God chose them in mercy (Ho 11:1-4), directed divine wrath against their oppressor, and made of them a nation. Given a place among kingdoms and empires, they naturally thought of themselves as God's favorites, expecting God's wrath to wipe out their enemies. How shocking to hear the prophetic accusation: It is you pious people who are now God's enemies, because you neglect the poor and forget justice. Against you is the divine wrath poured out![17]

115)   Sin, in the Bible, is rebellion against God. Through the history of Israel, God has clearly communicated the divine will, interpreted by the prophets, embodied in Jesus Christ, and contained in the scriptures. To turn against that holy will is sin. Other peoples might think of sin as undesirable conduct, such as a violation of tradition, a breaking of a social contract, disregard of an honored religious practice, or an error of judgment growing out of ignorance. But in the Bible sin is not primarily a matter of religious ceremonies or private morality. Rather, prophets and apostles alike stress justice and mercy as the very core of God's demand. Central to the divine will for humanity is the overcoming of alienation and conflict, the establishment of order, wholeness, and harmony—*shalom*. Failure to secure justice, to respond in love to one's neighbor, or to engage intentionally in reconciliation and peacemaking is not only a moral fault but is also an affront to God. In the Bible, ethics and religion are inextricably united. To sin against one's neighbor is to sin against God.

116)   God stands constantly ready to forgive when there is genuine repentance—a change of heart and of our ways. God's

intention is to move people everywhere to repentance. There is a divine strategy for redemption, but repentance which involves social as well as personal change is a prerequisite for forgiveness.

117)   The whole activity of God in human existence is expressed in Christian vocabulary in the word *grace.* The New Testament emphasizes grace as forgiveness, but never without repentance, nor without ethical concern.[18] Grace refers to the whole of God's love in action and is known only to those who know that God is love. God's grace is manifested in creation and in all of life, but above all in our redemption through the ministry of Jesus Christ.

118)   How can we who confess our faith in the living God of the Bible escape the burden of unbearable guilt attendant on the use of our nuclear arsenal? Lifting a phrase from the vocabulary of atomic warfare with its strategy of "preemptive strike," Jonathan Schell writes of "preemptive repentance"[19]—a change of mind and heart before the crime of using this weaponry can ever be committed. This notion calls us, in the spirit of the prophets and Jesus and the apostles, to forsake our evil ways and turn to the living God.

2. Jesus the Christ
119)   "As members of the Christian Church, we confess that Jesus is the Christ, the son of the living God, and proclaim him Lord and Savior of the world." In receiving candidates for baptism, we call on them to affirm the Good Confession (1 Ti 6:13; Mt 16:16) as their own declaration of faith and commitment. In affirming with the church through all the centuries that "Jesus is Lord" (Ro 10:9; Ac 2:36) we declare him supreme over every other authority which claims our loyalty. In love and dedication to him we acknowledge no higher sovereignty.

120)   Who was this Jesus of Nazareth whom we confess as Christ and Lord? He was a human being, beyond the shadow of a doubt. The faith of the earliest Christians is quite clear on this matter. They referred to him as "the man Christ Jesus" (1 Ti 2:5), as "Son of David" (Mt 1:1) from whom he "was descended . . . according to the flesh" (Rm 1:3), as one "born of woman" (Ga 4:4). Jesus spoke repeatedly of the Son of Man, rendered in modern terms as the New Being or the Human One; in these

50

passages the evangelists understood Jesus to have been speaking of himself. But though they insisted that he was truly and completely human, the early Christians were driven to say more of him.

121)   The Fourth Gospel begins with the majestic hymn: "In the beginning was the Word, and the Word was with God, and the Word was God" (Jn 1:1). Soon it reaches the climactic declaration, "The Word became flesh and dwelt among us" (1:14). Paul writes similarly, "God was in Christ reconciling the world" (2 Co 5:19). The unique event of which these passages speak Christians have long termed the Incarnation, the "enfleshment" or "inhumanizing" of God.

122)   Most commonly our discussions of the doctrine of Incarnation focus on the nature of Jesus Christ, whom the church, along with the Gospels, confesses as truly God and truly a man, as fully human and fully divine.

123)   This doctrine goes beyond the claim, staggering enough in itself, that in Jesus of Nazareth the eternal God entered our history in the life of one human being. Rather it declares that God entered fully and irrevocably into the totality of our human experience, into our human nature, into the closest possible union with the whole of humanity. That union continues forever unbroken and unbreakable; this is the meaning of *bodily* resurrection and ascension. God remains eternally and intimately enfleshed in our entire suffering humanity. Any action visited upon any person anywhere is therefore visited upon God. "As you did it to one of the least of these," the divine Judge says concerning his helpless sisters and brothers, "you did it to me" (Mt 25:40).

124)   In the face of the needy, the sufferer, the enemy, we see the face of the incarnate God. What we do to the needy, the sufferer, the enemy, we do to God. Moreover, our every action as Christians either expresses or denies the intention of the Christ who, in indwelling our humanity, lives not only in all other persons, but in each of us as well. Conversion to the way of Christ demands the radical change which follows our acknowledgement of this indwelling: "It is no longer I who live, but Christ who lives in me" (Ga 2:20). "To me to live is Christ" (Ph 1:21). The Christian life is a continuing effort to release the divine impulse through all that we say and do.

125)   In the Gospels the followers of Jesus customarily address him as Rabbi or Master. To take him as Teacher is an inescapable implication of our claim to be his disciples. A disciple is a follower, a learner, a student, an adherent, and then an advocate.

126)   We hail this Teacher as Prince of Peace. By his gospel he calls us to open our lives and submit our wills to the Reign of God. He bids us learn the blessedness of the meek, the compassionate, the makers of peace, the despised for his sake (Mt 5:5-12). He warns that his way is hard in contrast with the crowded road that leads to destruction (Mt 7:13-14). He counsels that a serious response to his call will evoke dissension and rejection on the part of our co-workers and friends and even members of our families. He faces us with hard decisions (Lk 14:26-27).

127)   To claim Jesus as Lord and Christ is also to take him as our Example. "It is enough for the disciple to be like the teacher, and the servant like the one who is served" (Mt 10:25). Sometimes it seems relatively easy and attractive to follow the pattern he gave—in being open to persons, in lifting up those who need a hand, in speaking up for the helpless and forgotten, even in giving our life for another. We may even find serenity and satisfaction in the emulation. At other times his example, like his teaching, seems beyond us—not only beyond our powers, but even beyond our inclinations. Before his ready acceptance of the lot of the Suffering Servant, his willingness to endure wrong but not to inflict wrong, his prayer on behalf of those who schemed against him and sent him to his death, we can only cry with Peter, "Depart from me, for I am a sinful man, O Lord" (Lk 5:8). But he does not depart; he forgives. Still he does not permit us any easy discipleship. Rather he insists, "Follow me" (Mk 1:17; Lk 5:10). "Take up your cross and follow me" (see Mt 16:24).

128)   We cannot shake off either the lure or the demand of this supreme example. Forever beyond us, yet ever ready to transform us into his likeness, he draws us toward himself (2 Co 3:18; Heb 12:1-2). As we work through the implications of our baptism, we accommodate our lives to the pattern he has set (Rm 6:5-11).

129)   We acknowledge Jesus Christ as the great reconciler whose supreme ministry was to restore peace between humanity and God by bringing us back from our rebellion against God and making it possible for us to be at one with our divine Parent. This reconciliation flows from Jesus Christ's atoning death on the cross (Ep 1:7-10; Col 1:15-20; 3:17-18). Restored to peace with God by the work of Christ, we are called as Christians to a ministry of reconciliation; this vocation involves bringing to repentance persons who are at enmity, so that they may become right with God and with one another (2 Co 5:16-21; Mt 5:9, 21-26).

130)   Confessing Jesus as the Christ, we are bound to ask: What direction do we find from him as we ponder the issues of nuclear war?

- If the incarnate Christ is forever one with all who suffer, with the victims of nuclear conflict and with those who perpetrate it, how does that affect our decisions on public policy?
- If Jesus Christ is our teacher, what do we learn from him regarding the way to peace?
- If Jesus Christ is our example, what does it mean to confess the Crucified One "Lord of all"? How does the foolishness of the cross become the power of God to save a generation on the verge of nuclear annihilation?
- If Jesus Christ the reconciler has called us to a ministry of reconciliation, how must we fulfill this vocation in a world of hostile nations whose reliance on nuclear weapons threatens the whole creation?

3. The Unity of the Spirit

131)   The Bible speaks frequently of the presence and activity of God's Spirit in human affairs. Though closely associated with revelation, the Spirit clearly transcends the narrow confines of formal religion and of a particular people. The early Christian community associated conversion with the gift of the Holy Spirit—a greater sensitivity to the Spirit's presence and responsiveness to the Spirit's guidance. The fruits of the Spirit were prized among them (Ga 5:22-23), and unity held a prominent place (Ep 4:1-7). Disciples have been particularly impressed by the explicit and insplicit affirmation of unity in the New Testament (Jn 17:20-21, 1 Co 12:12-13) and have

celebrated the role of the unity of the church as a foretaste of the unity which God wills for all of creation (Ep 1:1-10).

132) The missionary movement of the nineteenth century and the ecumenical movement of the twentieth have greatly helped to broaden our understanding of the unity of the Spirit by enlarging our experience. The Christian Church (Disciples of Christ) works intimately with churches of many names on six continents. We see them and ourselves as participating in that great "church of Christ upon earth" which Thomas Campbell declared "essentially, intentionally, and constitutionally one." We see that unity of Christ's followers given by the Holy Spirit, but still only imperfectly received, as sign and promise of the unity which God intends for all of humankind.

133) But we have scarcely begun to ask what the unity of the church means for us in the realm of ethics, especially in the case of war. The just war theory, when first taken over by the church, tacitly assumed a conflict between a Christian power (the later Roman Empire) and barbarian tribes beyond the limits of civilization, and the notion of crusading intensified the assumption. When later applied to conflicts between nation-states in Europe and America, this mindset tempted every so-called Christian nation to see itself as fighting God's battles and to look upon the enemy (even another nation sharing the Christian heritage of Western civilization) as a demonic power. In one war after another that process has involved self-deception, propaganda, and falsehood.

134) Now at the prospect of nuclear annihilation which threatens entire populations, we realize with a start that we Christians who proclaim ourselves one in Christ have been set against one another in a game of death by the claims of our various nations to unlimited sovereignty. How can we declare that their people and ours are God's good creation and simultaneously send nuclear missiles against them? Yet Jesus Christ has bought our freedom from the empty folly of our traditional ways (1 Pt 1:18, NEB). In that freedom we are called to offer the church as sign and promise of a reconciled humanity. How can we fulfill our vocation if we bring suffering and extinction on millions in the human family?

4. The Future God Offers

135)   The prophets, Jesus, and the authors of the New Testament books spoke frequently of God's impending future under such images as the Day of the Lord, the Last Day, the End. A significant branch of theology is called eschatology, the doctrine of last things (*eschata* in Greek, the language of the New Testament). Because certain premillennial groups occupy themselves with this theme in a way that seems unbalanced and irrational, many modern Disciples tend to avoid it. In doing so, we neglect an emphasis central to the thought of the New Testament and to the prayer which Jesus taught: "Thy kingdom come." Beyond the frenzied efforts to predict the end of the world by a certain date (a venture in which misguided Christians have been deceived century after century), what has the biblical doctrine of Last Things to teach us?

136)   Hope in God and in the triumph of God's purpose is the central thrust of biblical eschatology. Concern with the *ending* of history (the time, the manner) is minimal in scripture; concern with the *End* of history is a dominant theme. The End is God's goal for the entire enterprise, God's purpose in creation, the actualizing of *shalom*. Jesus' term for the End was God's reign, the kingdom of heaven. To him that reign was at hand, as near as the readiness of women and men to receive it (Mk 1:15). Most people, of course, were not ready, and they sent him to a cross. But in preaching Jesus as the Christ, the Messiah, the church continues to point toward the coming of God's new age.

137)   That vision of God's final purpose constantly waiting to break in upon us wherever human readiness can be found has shaped the Christian understanding of social responsibility through the centuries. The realization of how things ought to be presses upon the way things are in judgment and in hope. The gospel is good news for the poor and oppressed, bad news for the wealthy oppressor (Lk 6:20-26). From time to time a new glimpse of that vision has brought rapid social progress in a particular sector, the end of some ancient evil (slavery in the nineteenth century, legalized racial segregation in twentieth century America). The social vision of the early Disciples of Christ, as we have seen, centered (like that of many of their contemporaries) on the Millennium, the reign of Christ to be brought about by the evangelization of the world.

138)   Too often these days we think of the future by project-
ing present trends, and frequently that drives us to long for "the
good old days." Jesus by contrast did not pine for a golden past.
He knew that people in the present repeat pretty much the pattern of those in the long ago (Mt 24:37-39). But he did proclaim
God's future, the breaking in of the kingdom which it is God's
good pleasure to give (Lk 12:32). God's glorious future is the
world's supreme hope.

139)   How do we as Christians think responsibly about the
future? About our obligation to generations to come? About the
shaping of our present by the purpose of God? How does such
thinking bear on our struggle with the issues of nuclear war?

5. Summary
140)   The convictions to which we have referred here are
not trivial notions or marginal emphases. They are central elements in the Christian faith. With utmost seriousness, therefore, we ask ourselves: What do these theological convictions
say to us about conducting nuclear warfare? How can they
guide us in preventing nuclear war?

C. Essential Ethical Considerations

1. Thinking Through Our Choices
141)   Ethics is thinking about the reasons we make the
choices we do. Many of our choices are made on the basis of cus-
tom or habit. We decide without much reflection. Growing up
in a particular family and community provides us with a sense
of what is proper and improper behavior, of right and wrong
actions. Much of our moral conscience is shaped by our society.
Conformity to social convention is taken for granted as moral
behavior.

142)   Ethics raises questions about the motives, presuppositions, and values which *actually* influence our decision-
making. Ethics also raises questions about the motives, presuppositions, and values which *ought* to shape our decision-
making. Ethics helps us realize that in some circumstances our
personal motives and values may run counter to the socially acceptable customs of our family and community. Ethics helps us
make decisions on the basis of our particular personal beliefs

and values. Ethics helps us become more self-aware or self-critical in choosing a course of action closest to or consistent with our deeply held convictions. Ethics helps us maintain our integrity as persons.

143) *Christian* ethics is the effort to discern which motives, presuppositions, and values ought to influence our decision-making as followers of Jesus Christ. What difference does personal faith in Jesus Christ make in our decision-making? To what extent has our moral conscience been shaped by the gospel? Christian ethics helps us make decisions on the basis of motives, presuppositions, and values which are grounded in or consistent with the will of God as revealed in Jesus Christ. Christian ethics helps us maintain our integrity as Christians.

144) Most Christians in North America assume that the morals of their society are reliable and true. The socially approved ways of living are for the most part taken for granted and regarded as consistent with the will of God, even by those Christians who react to moral pluralism and permissiveness by seeking to recover the traditional customs of the past. Christian ethics is a self-critical approach for comparing social and personal values with the central affirmations and moral experiences of the Christian faith. Both contemporary and traditional moralities may receive mixed reviews from such a comparison. Some values of our society actually express the will of God, at least in a partial way; others must be identified as cultural "virtues" which have little compatability with the gospel of Jesus Christ. Christian ethics places the believer on guard not to assume uncritically that socially approved moral reasoning is the same as God's will.

145) The life of faith is a life of struggle. Jesus Christ is our measure. As his disciples, we stand under him as guide and judge in our decision-making. He is both Lord and Savior of each of us personally; he is also the Lord and Savior of the whole creation: nations, thrones, principalities, and powers. The life of faith is a struggle because of our human sin. The human propensity for self-justification, personal stability, and group acceptance causes us to accommodate to the social world in which we live. We resist critical analysis when we are comfortable. The testimony of the scriptures and the experience of the church affirm the radical nature of human sin. The gospel

imperative is to live as a child of God in all we do, but none of us measures up to this high calling. The life of Christian commitment and responsible decision-making is ever in tension with human sin and the prevailing patterns in society. There is no clear and easy road to Christian discipleship.

146)   In facing questions of Christian ethics it is helpful to remind ourselves that faithful, intelligent, and responsible Christians have not always agreed. This diversity of ethical viewpoints should be regarded as an asset rather than liability for the Christian life. It expresses the freedom which God has given to human beings as a part of the creation. At the same time it shows how God uses diverse persons and movements, even with apparent conflicts to accomplish the divine will in history. It cautions us against assuming that one particular ethical stance is the only one possible for a Christian.

2. Inadequate Responses to the Nuclear Question
147)   Faced with the complexities of the nuclear reality, some people feel powerless to do anything. When exposed to information about the potentially destructive results of a nuclear war, these people avoid or deny the problem. In a similar fashion some Americans, conditioned by the Vietnam and Watergate years, have lost confidence in the democratic values and institutions of the nation. Such a judgment leads to indifference or cynicism. In either case, withdrawal from the political process cannot be justified for the Christian.

148)   There are other people who seek a simplistic solution to the nuclear threat. These people deny or avoid the complexities of the nuclear reality. It is not uncommon to hear well-meaning Christians desiring to apply sayings such as "turn the other cheek" or "the Golden Rule" to the nuclear scene. Christian ethicists through the centuries have cautioned the church that such moral wisdom may provide guidelines for interpersonal relationships, but is inadequate for large-scale social problems. It takes a great deal of effort, imagination, and guidance by the Holy Spirit to apply such maxims to relations among nations. To appeal to the familiar sayings from scripture may be the beginning of the quest, but these certainly offer little counsel in regard to specific national policies, defense strategies, and the nuclear reality. Neither cynicism nor simplistic approaches will do. These are inadequate for faithful people.

3. On Using Scripture

149)   Disciples of Christ see themselves as a "people of the Book." The Bible is central to our faith and life. Yet, like all people, we approach our study of the Bible from a particular historical and social setting. Our perspectives are conditioned by family, neighborhood, race, class, sex, education, occupation, and personality. Our perspective influences what we see in the Bible and in the world, and shapes our response to that perception of reality.

150)   To further complicate matters, a characteristic of our sinful or fallen state is the human inclination to justify our own point of view. When approaching the scriptures uncritically, we tend to see what we want to see and thus to find "biblical" sanction for what is familiar and traditional for us.

151)   Further complications arise when we approach scripture for guidance on a moral question. The Bible gives "mixed signals" on some significant issues which it addresses directly. A recent study examines passages in the Bible dealing with slavery, the Sabbath, war, and women.[20] It concludes that there is no single point of view in scripture on any of these four moral questions. The Bible, written by different persons at different times in different socio-political circumstances, contains differing viewpoints on each one.

152)   An awareness of these facts calls for serious effort as we seek to interpret scripture. This effort includes using historical and literary approaches to our study of the Bible. The study is to be pursued within the community of faith, ecumenically inclusive, and open to the guidance of the Holy Spirit. Further, as Christians together engage in the study and interpretation of scripture we must acknowledge our own theological affirmations and historical conditioning. Our different situations in life influence the passages and biblical themes we select for moral guidance.

4. The Openness of Disciples

153)   Earlier in the historical portion of our document (Chapter I, Part B) we indicated some distinctive characteristics of Disciples of Christ. Mindful of this tradition, we now approach the question of nuclear threat in light of the compelling biblical message and our basic Christian convictions.

154)   No Christian is bound to one particular orientation, either to scripture or to the world. Disciples of Christ have been vigorous proponents of openness to new wisdom. Renewal of life in personhood, in the congregation and in the larger society is a value central to our religious heritage. We are aware that new information and new life experience can reorient us. We are aware that there is new insight from the Bible, that the Word of God is an active, creative, renewing force which can turn us around. The One to whom the Bible points is not limited by our human condition. New truth breaks in upon as as we are receptive to the Holy Spirit.

New occasions teach new duties.
Time makes ancient good uncouth.[21]

155)   In striving for a faithful response to a moral question, especially to an issue related to modern technology and which the Bible does not address, Disciples are open to a number of considerations.

156)   The empirical and pragmatic approach which characterizes Disciples necessitates learning as much as we can about the actual situation in which our choices are made. We need to have competent social, economic, political, military, and technological analyses. We need to be aware of the honest differences among informed specialists in these areas. The Christian has a moral obligation to be as informed as possible on the question at hand. The issues are complicated, but not beyond comprehension.

157)   Second, we need to be aware of the moral insights on particular ethical questions, in this case the nuclear reality and the quest for peace, which other peoples hold. We have much to learn from the moral wisdom which is part of the larger human experience.

158)   Third, there needs to arise an interplay or dialogue of the biblical and theological with nonbiblical information and insights. This interplay may be likened to a conversation in which various persons contribute and respond. Such a conversation is not private. This conversation goes on within the church where biblical insights and theological affirmations relate decision-making to the Christian faith. Decisions on the issues of nuclear weaponry and nuclear policy cannot be made

on the basis of the Bible alone nor, for the Christian, can they be made without reference to the ethical values and moral wisdom present within the Bible, theology, and the experience of the church. The scriptures, especially insofar as they reveal Jesus Christ, are normative for Christians. The community of faith, the church, the body of Christ, is the immediate context in which ethical issues are examined, options clarified, and decisions made. Decisions on moral issues by Christians are personal, but not private.

5. Considerations for Disciples in Response to the Nuclear Question

159)   Disciples of Christ carry in their tradition a certain theological understanding of the American nation. Both Thomas and Alexander Campbell shared a vision of the United States as a country with a divine vocation. Such a religious perception has been a strong and abiding motif in the national self-understanding. Disciples have participated, along with others, in this mode of communal self-consciousness. The national experiment in liberty was believed by the nation's founders and by the Disciples' founders to be a fulfillment of divine providence. The nation was under God's guidance and God's judgment. Alexander Campbell saw the religious movement he led as the harbinger of a "new political and religious order of society known as the Millennium."[22] The purpose of a Christian America was to extend the reign of Christ throughout the world. This kind of conviction stood behind much of the missionary activity of the nineteenth and twentieth centuries. Although this kind of national self-understanding could degenerate into the concept of "Manifest Destiny" and uncritical chauvinism, the perspective of the early Disciples kept sight of the transcendence of God. Not just any national policy could be blessed. National life and policy are significant but not ultimate.

160)   Central to contemporary Disciples thought is the theological significance of human society. Human beings have both the need and the capacity to develop culture and social order. Persons come to selfhood in a social matrix. Family, school, church, work, and community provide the settings in which persons take on identity and manifest their potential as children of God. Biblical passages and theological affirmations point to the governance of God over the whole of creation including human societies. God wills the proper ordering of

human relationships so that personal growth and mutual benefit may be enjoyed by all persons. This perception of positive theological significance in human society establishes a basis for Christian citizenship. Involvement in political process and the formation of public policy are expressions of faithful witness to the ethical imperative of love, justice, liberty, human rights, and peace.

161) Disciples have a tradition of prophetic witness to the social problems of the day. Alexander Campbell spoke out his adamant objection to the War with Mexico. In 1828 he stood for election to the Constitutional Convention in Virginia in the hope of ameliorating the problem of slavery. Preston Taylor led black Disciples in the quest for full and equal participation in the life of church and society. By organizing a convention of black Disciples in 1917 he encouraged all Disciples to take a fresh and honest look at the particular challenges and opportunities presented by membership of blacks within the church since the beginning of the movement. Disciples women, meanwhile, had long been involved with the needs of society. Through the Christian Woman's Board of Missions they sent women and men overseas to evangelize and to establish schools, hospitals, and orphanages; in the homeland, in addition to founding new congregations, they conducted programs serving ethnic minorities, persons trapped in rural poverty, immigrants, and students in state universities. Carry A. Nation and Ida B. Wise Smith gained national prominence in the long campaign to control the liquor traffic. Other Disciples leaders addressed these and other social questions.[23] The church participates in national life as a shaper of personal moral consciousness and as moral conscience of the community. Justice and peace have long been paramount imperatives in Disciples tradition. Ethics is more than personal. Faithful witness is concerned with the whole of life, including the bearing of public policy on justice and peace.

162) Disciples of Christ in Canada and the United States are part of the super-rich and super-powerful nations of the world. The tremendous influence of these nations for world stability and development or for instability and disaster increases the obligations of citizenship. Given our commitment to justice and peace which we acknowledge as Christians, the need for an informed and responsible participation in the formation of

public policy is crucial. Democratic institutions require citizen participation. As Christian citizens we have a moral obligation to be informed, to debate the available options, and to act in ways which influence political decision toward the fulfillment of human rights, justice and peace—domestic and global.

163)   The nuclear reality is awesome. Global destruction is the probable consequence of a general nuclear war. The possibilities of a technical malfunction or of a miscalculation by government or military leaders could precipitate a nuclear exchange. Strategies of "launch on warning" and "use or lose" (nuclear weapons) preclude reasonable inquiry and composed judgment about any incident. Retaliatory nuclear reactions are already programmed. In such an event the entire world could suffer devastation. Civilization, the fragile product of centuries of human effort, with its complex economic, social and political institutions, could be obliterated. The death of innocent peoples violates biblical value placed on life. Destruction of the environment and of the cultural inheritance violates the biblical demand for stewardship of the earth and its fruits.

164)   The enormous sums of money and resources spent on the arms race offend our sensibilities toward the hungry and poor of the world. The amount of money spent on armaments is out of balance when compared with efforts to alleviate hunger, poverty, and disease—domestic and global. The biblical priorities clearly admonish the faithful to identify with and show concern for the poor and oppressed.

165)   Because love *(agape)* characterizes the response which Christians are to make to God's grace, it is incumbent on the faithful to translate that love into action. Such action addresses social institutions and public policies in addition to the way in which we deal with persons face to face. Justice is the way we express love in social relationships. To the extent that justice and love are imperative for the faithful, they provide the central moral guidelines for decision-making. *Shalom*, as God's gift, is the anticipated culmination of love and justice. Expressing paramount concern for the sanctity of life, human dignity, human rights, and stewardship of the creation, these guidelines function as compelling moral imperatives for Christians. Our task is to bring them to bear on the nuclear threat.

166)   Since ethical decision-making is the responsibility of every Christian, the panel considers it inappropriate to do other people's ethical thinking for them. At this point, however, we do challenge our readers to the urgent task of engaging the nuclear issue in the light of the history, biblical witness, theological principles, and ethical considerations we have presented up to this point. To aid in that process we set forth the following affirmations and questions.

6. Affirmations and Questions to Guide Ethical Choices

167)   *Disciples value personal integrity and the freedom to make up one's own mind.*
   - How free are we in our ethical choices? Is our judgment truly independent, or do we decide like others in our social setting?
   - Are we free to differ?
   - Are we free to accept others who differ from us?

168)   *Disciples value knowledge and openness to new information.*
   - How informed are we?
   - Have we put forth the effort to learn all we can about the nuclear question?
   - Are we familiar with the current national debate over nuclear policy?

169)   *Disciples affirm that the Bible is central to faithful living.*
   - What bearing do our convictions about God, the creation, justice, *shalom*, and the covenant have on our ethical choices?
   - What bearing does the Lordship of Jesus Christ have on our position toward nuclear war?

170)   *Disciples believe in the fellowship of the congregation and in the presence of the Holy Spirit wherever two or three are gathered together in the name of Jesus Christ.*
   - Has the issue of nuclear war been studied and discussed within the fellowship of the congregation?
   - Has the guidance of the Holy Spirit been sought in the search for faithful witness to the nuclear question?

171) *Disciples have a concern for public policy.*
- In what ways does the current policy of our nation protect or jeopardize the prospects for justice and peace?
- What are the present options for our society? What are the foreseeable consequences of these options?

172) *Disciples, along with other Christians, have been guided in the past by the classical options on war.* Developed, as we have noted, in situations far different from our own, these classical options may provide us with widely tested criteria as we form our own judgments about nuclear war.

173) *Should we follow the path of pacifism?* Believing that the "Prince of Peace" would never have engaged in battle, the early Christians proclaimed that taking the life of another human being was not compatible with the teachings of the church. Ancient rulers observed, "Christians would rather be killed than kill." Pacifism does not imply an acceptance of evil, nor does it suggest that evil should not be resisted. Evil should be overcome with good. Pacifism affirms that nonviolent resistance has longer-lasting effect for good than does violence.
- Is the preservation of life a greater value than the preservation of freedom or justice?
- Would unilateral renunciation of any use or possession of nuclear weapons invite a nonpacifistic nuclear nation to pursue expansionist aggression without fear of retribution?
- Would not persistence in nonviolent resistance of an enemy result in eventual *shalom* without the terrible cost of nuclear war?

174) *Should we follow the path of the just war?* Responsible Christian thinkers have concluded that the existence of certain conditions justifies the resort to war. The just war theory seeks to limit and control both the frequency of war and its scope. It implies that peace, i.e., the absence of conflict, is not necessarily the highest good, that other values (such as freedom and justice) may rank even higher. Let us recall that in Christian thought a war is considered just when *all* six of the following criteria are met:
1. The war must be declared by a legitimate authority.

2. It must be carried out with a right intention; its purpose must be to promote peace.
3. The war must be undertaken only as a last resort. It must be a last resort to resolving conflict.
4. It must be waged on the basis of the principle of proportionality. The relationship between ends and means must be proportionate.
5. The war must have a reasonable chance of success.
6. It must be waged with all the moderation possible. Particular care must be taken to see that civilian noncombatants and prisoners of war are not tortured or killed.

In this nuclear age, we must ask:
- Can Christians accept weapons of indiscriminate mass destruction of both civilian populations and the environment on the basis of the just war?
- Could a nuclear first strike against an enemy be justified for Christians?
- Are the consequences of nuclear war proportionate to the desired goal of peace?
- Are not the values of freedom and justice worth the risk of nuclear war?
- Can a *nuclear* war be a just war?

175)   *Can we find a new path in this nuclear age?*
Biblical faith provides theological affirmations and ethical demands which are constant throughout history. Although love, justice, and peace have been variously conceived and variously applied, they continue to guide Christians in their decision-making. Many Christians are seeking for new ethical guidance to the question of war in a nuclear age. There is an increasing opinion that conventional moral wisdom regarding war is obsolete. In the search for new paths, the Panel notes the growing appeal of a position identified as nuclear pacifism. Nuclear pacifism is the disavowal of nuclear weapons. Freedom allows for new choices for action. Whatever we decide, we are called to do so in faithfulness to the abiding ethical demands of love, justice, and peace. When these obligations of faith are applied to the realities of the nuclear threat, do they move us toward new responses, new possibilities?
- Is not nuclear pacifism a responsible and realistic option?
- Are there other faithful ways?

66

IV. Making Peace in
a Nuclear Age

A. *Taking Up Our Christian Responsibility*

1. Keeping Faith with the Vision.
176)   While there are obvious political, economic, social, and technological dimensions to the issues of nuclear war, it must be recognized that the issues posed are first and foremost of a religious and ethical nature. Through the scriptures we have received a vision of God's intention to overcome all hostility and alienation, and to bring *shalom* to all creation. Our calling is to be faithful to that divine revelation and that vision. From the standpoint of biblical faith, nuclear issues are religious issues. The vision of God's concern for human suffering and God's wrath against those who cause oppression and destruction must become our guiding vision if we would claim to be God's people.

177)   Keeping faith with the vision involves a renewed commitment to Bible study, the cultivation of spiritual integrity, and a deeper rootage in the faith of our forebears. It calls for reconciliation with our enemies and a renewed sense of penitence. Such penitence acknowledges our responsibility both individually and corporately for many of the circumstances which have brought us to the brink of nuclear destruction. It demands an intentional and persistent cultivation of a deeper spirituality, appropriate to those who have glimpsed the vision of the world God wills and promises. In our intercessions we Christians should pray daily for that peace, justice, and unity made known to us in the vision of *shalom*. In addition to the pastoral concern for healing the hurts of our own members which is so often, and rightly, expressed in the public petitions of the church, we are called to offer prayers for all people, espe-

cially leaders in high positions, that the world may be at peace. Jesus bade us pray for our enemies and remember the poor and the hungry. Christian spirituality requires more involvement with the world, not less, even in prayer.

2. Engaging the Issues

178)   If the church is to deal effectively with the moral questions of this nuclear age, we must deal directly and concretely with the issues which it poses. The rich heritage of biblical themes, theological doctrines and ethical principles must be brought into direct encounter with the specific and concrete questions of the nuclear age. This will require sustained study, the organization of discussion and reflection groups in local congregations, the serious consideration of materials produced by persons of diverse religious traditions, and the careful use of studies and documents which originate in other parts of the world. An important dimension of this study is to be found in keeping well informed regarding discussions and debates taking place within specialized circles of leaders in politics, economics, science, and medicine.

179)   No vague and abstract solutions will be useful. Few if any of the particular issues are subject to simple analysis or lead to an easy conclusion. The church is called to a much more sophisticated level of understanding than it has sometimes shown and to a thorough grappling with the particular issues posed in the nuclear age.

3. Confessing Ignorance and Respecting Differences

180)   Discussions in religious circles are sometimes curtailed or impoverished by a climate of rigid dogmatism, of echoing traditional cliches, or of assuming a posture of moralistic superiority. Certainly this nuclear age calls for a different climate. Now we must readily acknowledge the newness and complexity of the issues before us. We must admit that the easy answers of the past do not respond to the difficult questions of the present. Skills of listening are as important as skills of speaking. An openness to face new facts and struggle with honest differences among sincere believers must be cultivated.

181)   Together we move out into unfamiliar territory without proven and tested maps, and without adequate ability to foresee the possible consequences of alternative proposals for

action. All of us walk more by faith than by sight, and the enterprise in which we are engaged calls both for great faith and great humility. In such a climate, the dialogue can take place, growth in understanding is possible, the bonds of the Christian community can be strengthened even as they are tested by our differences. Together we can demonstrate the faith, not by avoiding the hard and difficult issues, but by affirming our common faith and joining hands and minds in a common search to know and do God's holy will in these awesome times.

4. Making Decisions as Christians

182)   As members of churches we are also members of other groups and institutions—political parties, economic organizations, regional and national associations. Each of these constituencies has its vested interests, its value systems, and its authority figures. We cannot deny our participation in these groups; in fact, it is of the utmost importance that these memberships be acknowledged, lest we become unconsciously possessed by them. But the challenge before us as followers of Jesus Christ is to make conscious decisions as Christians, honoring our commitment to him above the claims and assumptions of every other authority.

183)   Accordingly we must test our attitudes, positions, and actions by the biblical, theological, and ethical components of the Christian faith. Personal attitudes toward other peoples must be Christlike, lifestyles and values must be brought into harmony with Christian convictions, and all areas of life, including economic and political dimensions, must be tested by our understanding of the gospel. The ethical issues posed by the nuclear age sooner or later pose direct personal challenges to each of us. We participate in the political process. We invest personal funds and engage in other economic endeavors. We seek to influence the activities and direction of secular groups to which we belong. We advocate changes in public policy. All these must reflect a consciously held Christian ethic and a serious intent to achieve consistency in witnessing to that ethic.

184)   Not only do we make decisions as individual Christians, but the church as church is called to speak its mind and exercise its teaching responsibility for its members and for the general society. Across the centuries, churches have elaborated ethical positions concerning the reality of war. Today, we face

new realities which demand that the church review its posture of the past and speak with clarity in the present. An atmosphere conducive to such decisions by the church must be actively created and sustained. The church must speak clearly—first to its own members, and then to the general society. In addressing these emerging nuclear issues, the church reflects the biblical position of the unity of all of life and of the sovereignty of God over all of creation. For the church to speak to the issues of faith and morality in a nuclear age is not only its right, but, from a biblical perspective, its obligation.

5. Addressing Public Policy

185)   The issues posed in the nuclear age must be dealt with in the arena of public policy. The decisions on policies which lead to life or to death are the responsibility of all of us, but especially of those who hold positions of responsibility and authority in government. Supporting or opposing proposed public policies is a major responsibility of individual Christians and of the church corporately. Where Christians gather in congregations or in assemblies of broader geographical dimensions, it is imperative that the emerging issues of war and peace receive attention and that the voice of the church be heard clearly. Joint study and ecumenical action are imperative in our times. As a worldwide community, the church must engage in a worldwide Christian dialogue so that the judgments and opinions of Christians in any particular place may be informed by the insights of the total community of faith. Only in this way can the people of God truly be a "light to the nations" and fulfill their calling from God (Is 49:6).

B. Choosing a Position on Nuclear Issues

186)   Without attempting to discuss military strategy in any technical way, it is possible to suggest a range of alternative policies which are commonly advocated. About each of these the Panel's concern is with its ethical implications. We therefore raise certain questions confronting the Christian conscience and then offer our own judgment. We print the conclusions of the Panel in bold-faced type.

1. Maintaining a Total Arsenal

187)   Some political and military leaders believe that the

70

defense establishment should develop and maintain a full range of weapons—conventional, chemical, and nuclear. Technological feasibility is the only limit on what may be devised or used. The overriding consideration is to maintain sufficient military strength to enable the nation and its allies to dominate in any contest. Tending to recognize no essential difference between nuclear weapons and conventional arms, proponents of this policy call for a nuclear first-strike capability in order to minimize the likelihood of hostile action by the enemy.

- Can a convincing Christian rationale be advanced in favor of reliance on weapons of mass destruction?
- To the Christian, does "might make right"?
- Is there no qualitative difference between nuclear weapons and conventional arms?
- What security is offered by a total arsenal which, if used, would result in the destruction of those it is set up to defend?

188)   Among Disciples responding as individuals to a poll conducted during the General Assembly at San Antonio in 1983, the overwhelming majority (85 percent) saw nuclear weapons as essentially different from conventional means of making war. **The Panel believes that the current policy of the superpowers, as each seeks military superiority and the continued enhancement of nuclear capability, is wholly unacceptable. The policy results in both the stockpiling of weapons and the development, testing, and production of new devices for destruction. It violates the proper economic priorities of the nations, misdirects the intellectual efforts of research scholars, and abuses the oppressed. The panel rejects this option.**

2. Mutual Assured Destruction

189)   Since World War II the superpowers have relied on the policy of Mutual Assured Destruction (MAD) as the most reliable guarantee against the outbreak of nuclear conflict. Under the name of deterrence, this policy has had mixed results: It appears to have staved off nuclear war, but it has resulted in a dramatic escalation of the arms race. Yet many realists in public affairs consider this policy a success; they advocate it, not without uneasiness, as the safest course before the nation.

- Can Christians regard mutual assured destruction of the enemy and our own nation (and perhaps of the

71

earth's capacity to sustain life) as a morally acceptable national policy?
- Are sufficient safeguards built into the military
procedures to prevent unintended outbreak of nuclear war?
- How is the plausibility of this policy affected as increasing numbers of nations acquire nuclear capability and even nuclear weapons?

190)   The Panel notes that current policies relying on
mutual assured destruction have not increased international
security nor advanced the progress of efforts toward the limita-
tion of nuclear arms. **The Panel stands categorically opposed to
any deterrent strategy which threatens mass annihilation by indiscriminate targeting of civilian populations.**

3. Limited Nuclear Warfare

191)   Some advocate the development of new technologies
for the purpose of limiting nuclear destruction by the capacity
to target specific military objectives within a precise range.
Success of this policy depends on choosing the smallest target
possible for attaining a specific military objective, thus giving
the enemy a chance to negotiate an armistice before widespread annihilation occurs. The Panel believes this notion is
lacking in realism.

- Given the prevailing pattern for the deployment of
nuclear weapons and military establishments generally, is it possible to attack these without bringing
death to great numbers of civilians?
- Is it likely that nuclear war can be limited if both
sides possess nuclear weapons?

192)   While the indirect or unintended consequence of
causing civilian casualties in a nuclear attack on a military target may seem less morally objectionable than all-out nuclear
war, the outcome would not likely be so simple. Military facilities and industrial sites are often found in the midst of cities; civilian casualties would almost certainly be comparable to those
in a deliberate counterpopulation attack, especially if, as seems
inevitable, the attack should provoke a substantial exchange.
The chaos inherent in the nature of nuclear war makes it ex-
tremely unlikely that a reasonable, logical, and systematic
strategy for limiting such a war can prevail. **The Panel therefore believes that the idea of limited nuclear war is a dangerous**

and destabilizing concept. It would most likely provoke a massive retaliatory attack, followed by unlimited counterattack, the result being utter devastation. Thus it would render meaningless any presumed deterrent effect in the counterbalancing of nuclear stockpiles.

4. Threatened Use as Deterrent

193)   Some moralists as well as military and diplomatic leaders defend the *possession* of targeted nuclear weapons as a deterrent against first use by the enemy and argue this policy as essential realism while efforts proceed to negotiate the reduction or elimination of nuclear arms. They maintain that the threat has effectively inhibited the resort to nuclear warfare and that the possession of nuclear weapons is therefore justified under certain conditions.

- Morally, is there a difference between the *threat* to use nuclear weapons and their actual use?
- Is it likely that the superpowers can avoid the multiplying of nuclear weapons if they follow the policy of threatened use as deterrent?

194)   At the 1983 San Antonio General Assembly, 42 percent of the respondents to a questionnaire submitted by the Panel considered "possession of nuclear arms morally justified in context of action towards arms control and disarmament." Almost an equal number (39 percent) said "No" to this option; 19 percent were undecided. Those justifying possession of nuclear arms hold that deterrence may be morally permissible as a *means* toward the end of nuclear control, reduction in armaments of all kinds, and negotiated settlements of international disputes, but reject it as a strategic goal *in itself*. Opponents believe that the very existence of nuclear weapons presents a morally unacceptable threat to the continuance of the human family and the rest of God's creation.

195)   The Panel believes that a serious evaluation of this policy involves much more than an acknowledgment that it seems to have averted a nuclear holocaust thus far. Under this policy, the nuclear arms race has continued unabated. Not only have weapons increased in sophistication and quantity, but the number of nations having nuclear capability, openly or secretly, continues to grow. With each increase in stockpiles and in membership in the nuclear club, the possibility also in-

creases that nuclear war will be triggered by a misreading of detections systems, computer malfunction, terrorist take-over of military command and control posts, or other unforeseen developments. These systems inevitably contain a first-strike capability, and world opinion overwhelmingly condemns the mere thought of exercising this option. A further liability is the diversion of massive amounts of resources away from programs of human services and toward the production, deployment, and maintenance of nuclear arsenals. Making the threat of nuclear reprisal a keystone of foreign policy has enhanced the role of military officials, at the expense of civilian influence, in the formulation of governmental policy. In maintaining the capability of immediate nuclear reprisal, programmed for instantaneous and quasi-automatic response, we have surrendered the ultimate control of our actions to decisions made by others. Since the very idea of deterrence presumes that the nuclear weapons will, in fact, be used, possession necessarily implies the intention to use them. For Christians this raises the question put by Jesus in the Sermon on the Mount: Is not intention to commit an act the moral equivalent of the act itself? The Panel concludes that whatever short-term benefit might be claimed for this policy, the long-term consequences are overwhelmingly negative. We believe that an urgent program of disarmament by all nations should be given the highest priority and that the policy of nuclear deterrence should be abandoned at the earliest possible moment.

5. Reduction of Nuclear Armaments

196)   A large body of opinion advocates the reduction of nuclear armaments. A nuclear freeze, i.e., an agreement to cease the further production, testing, and deployment of nuclear weapons, is generally viewed as a step in this process. Most proponents of this position insist on multilateral agreements and mutual verification of compliance as essential ingredients of such a policy. While the mutual reduction of arsenals is highly attractive, it poses difficult questions. Does reduction mean actually lowering available destructive power and the number of warheads—or only the number of vehicles? Does a build-down scheme—an agreement to destroy, say, two nuclear weapons for each new one deployed—actually reduce the equation for destruction, or does new technology provide as much firepower in one new weapon as in two old ones?

197)   Some thoughtful persons advocate that the nations, multilaterally or even unilaterally, pledge themselves to no first use of nuclear weapons. Others believe the dangers of nuclear war to be so great that they advocate unilateral reduction of atomic weapons as a gesture of good faith and a means of encouraging other nations to take a similar step. Some call for the total elimination of nuclear arms, ideally by multilateral agreement, but by unilateral action if necessary.

- What is the most responsible procedure for reducing or eliminating nuclear arms?
- What effect would unilateral reduction of nuclear arms by one of the superpowers likely have on the other?
- Is nuclear pacifism any less realistic than the other options that have been presented?

198)   **Because of the ominous implications of any crossing of the nuclear threshold, especially in the present global political climate, the Panel strongly urges that the United States pledge no first use of nuclear weapons. Such a pledge has been made by the Soviet Union. The Panel advocates the reduction of nuclear armaments with the understanding that the ultimate goal should be the elimination of nuclear weapons everywhere and that negotiations for mutual arms reduction should be stepped up. The Panel supports immediate, mutually verifiable agreements to halt production, testing, and deployment of nuclear weapons. The Panel also concludes that no use of nuclear arms can meet the requirements for a just war. We therefore advocate nuclear pacifism.**

6. Decisions for Communities and Individuals
199)   Any realistic effort to cut back production of nuclear weapons and reduce the magnitude of nuclear stockpiles must take into account the vested power of the military-technological complex (paragraphs 55-56). In scores of communities which depend for their prosperity on industries engaged in the manufacture of weapons systems or their components, thousands of workers draw their paychecks from the corporations involved. In a time of economic uncertainty the award of a new contract causes civic celebration, while the announcement of a cutback spells layoffs and even long-term unemployment. Increasingly, major universities rely on contracts with the defense department for large-scale funding of new research. Members

of Congress, intent on reelection, vie with one another to secure new appropriations for military bases or weapons manufacturers in their districts. Any significant change from the current military posture will necessarily involve major economic readjustments, though it is reasonable to hold that vast funds being spent on the means of destruction, if redirected to more positive uses, could greatly improve the quality of human life around the world.[24] In any case, Christians who work at the nuclear issue will have to struggle with the ambiguities in our current patterns of economic dependence on war industry.

- As Christians can we justify the economic dependence of our communities and members on the manufacture and deployment of nuclear weapons systems?
- How can we deal responsibly with the problems of our members and communities which will be incurred in cutting back the production of nuclear arms?

200)   **The Panel deplores our pattern of economic dependence on the war industry. Convinced that greater economic health for the world will follow a reversal of the arms race, we call upon the churches to join with other public-spirited groups in a creative search for new and constructive types of enterprise to sustain the economic health of our communities and of the world.**

201)   The many issues we have discussed up to this point have dealt largely with matters of national policy. As Christians we have an obligation to express our convictions on such matters by the exercise of our responsibilities as citizens. This might include joining the public debate, voting for candidates whose position on these questions accords with our own, running ourselves for public office. Quite apart from such engagement in politics, however, each of us is faced with personal decisions which we dare not make without full consideration of our commitments as disciples of Christ.

- If called by my government, should I as a Christian serve under arms?
- If inducted into the armed forces, should I accept an assignment which involves the operation of nuclear systems?

- As a civilian, should I accept work in the development and manufacture of nuclear arms?
- Should I invest in a corporation which produces nuclear arms?
- As a taxpayer should I withhold from payment that portion of my income tax which funds nuclear weaponry (and be prepared to accept the consequences)?
- Should I engage in public demonstrations protesting against the manufacture and deployment of nuclear weapons?
- Should I take part in acts of civil disobedience, such as trespassing in antinuclear demonstrations (and be prepared to accept the consequences)?

While the ethical issues confronted by Christians in a society preparing for nuclear war are highly complex and sometimes ambiguous, every Christian decides these hard questions either by making a firm and deliberate choice or by not deciding and thus going along with prevailing policy. The General Assembly of the Christian Church (Disciples of Christ) has repeatedly taken action to support the ministry of chaplains to persons in the military services and to uphold the rights of persons who for reasons of conscience refuse to bear arms or serve in the armed forces.[25] It has not, however, given counsel on all the issues raised here.

202)   The Panel affirms the responsibility of Christians to discuss such issues together, to reach intentionally Christian decisions, to uphold one another in the rights of conscience, and to pray for one another. The Panel believes that the church in its general manifestation should also defend the right of conscience for citizens who protest their government's policy to involve them in acts of nuclear war or preparation for it.

C. Improving Global Relationships

203)   As nations across the earth seem bent on war and destruction, the dread nuclear missile stands as a terrible symbol, both the product of the nations' fears and the cause of new apprehensions. In this world of violence and conflict where the threat of annihilation looms, the appeal for peace rises in unceasing cry. By an incredible paradox, humanity yearns for

peace yet continues to regard the capacity to make war as the way to pursue peace. Under such circumstances, it is not enough to concentrate solely on preventing an exchange of missiles. To lessen the prospect of nuclear cataclysm, women and men of goodwill everywhere must find ways of lowering the tensions among the nations. The improvement of global relationships is a major task for Christians in our time.

1. Practicing Moderation and Goodwill

204)   Technological advances in war-making capability have not brought us closer to peace or to understanding the things that make for peace. The competition of the arms race strains relations among the nations to the breaking point. The rhetoric of confrontation seems to have replaced the language of diplomacy, with international name-calling substituted for reasoned discussion. Sovereign nations claim ultimate authority to make decisions in their own self-interest, with little regard for the needs and interests of others and, too often, not even "a decent respect to the opinions of mankind."[26] Like Goliaths who have never encountered their David, the antagonists imitate belligerent neighborhood bullies, relying on intimidation and the dominance of might to make right. Recently there have been signs of a slight improvement in relationships between the superpowers. Beginning with Andrei Gromyko's visit to the White House in the fall of 1984, the U.S.A. and the U.S.S.R. have agreed to reopen negotiations on arms control and disarmament. Whether these talks will bring about a lessening of hostilities remains to be seen.

205)   Relying on the threat of war to keep the peace has not helped the nations discover alternative methods for resolving conflicts and reducing tensions. The Panel believes that reliance on preparation for war as the basis for peacekeeping is essentially a logic of fear, which can never be the foundation of a just and sustainable world order. God's peace requires much more than the avoidance of war. Fear may prevent the outbreak of hostilities in the short term, but at the cost of continually nudging upward the levels of military preparedness, much as a drug addict needs a higher and higher dosage in a desperately futile and self-destructive attempt to attain that tantalizingly elusive sense of well-being and peace. It is clear that such a course of action offers no hope for the future.

206)   From our own history we have learned that our former enemies are not identified by any truly innate qualities of depravity such as we once perceived in the hated foe. Rather, the attribution of such qualities to particular peoples is subject to the fickleness of political relationships. It is time to shift from thinking which undertakes to keep the peace by strategies of ethnic caricature, fear, and intimidation. Our common peril demands a new pattern of thinking which finds the roots of our reciprocal hostility toward each other and searches for ways to change those conditions in order to build a more just and peaceful world.

207)   Culture and history are major influences in shaping the assumptions on which people rely to interpret their world and to give meaning to their personal experiences. Only as we apprehend this fact can we hope to understand ourselves or any other people. Then we can begin to perceive why the things we say and do arouse such fear and hostility in others, and to explain to them why their words and actions give rise to hatred and suspicion within us. Such a strategy of trying to understand the enemy will not magically transform hostile relationships, but it can start us toward the cultivation of goodwill, mutual acceptance, and trust. The creation of trust between peoples of different cultures and national traditions is not a short-term task, but the vision of God's *shalom* insistently beckons us to persist.

2. New Directions in Foreign Policy

208)   Once we have committed ourselves to a tone of moderation in our dealings with other nations and have undertaken to develop better understanding, we can move into more constructive policies in dealing with them. The Panel recommends several elements in such a course.

209)   *Restraining the Race in Conventional Arms.* While the nuclear arms race poses the most dramatic threat to the future of humanity, it is part of a larger contest in which the nations strive to outdo one another amassing weapons of every kind. New technological advances make conventional arms constantly more destructive, thus deepening the climate of fear. To gain an advantage nations are once again turning to the development of chemical weapons, breaking a moratorium on production which had been observed since 1969. It is not just

the superpowers that are caught up in the logic of fear. Global military spending now exceeds $800 billion annually (in terms of constant 1981 dollars). The international arms trade increased more than 70 percent from 1972 to 1982 ($20.2 billion in 1972; $34.4 billion in 1982) according to the U.S. Arms Control and Disarmament Agency. Over three-quarters of the weaponry is sold to developing countries, with the largest suppliers being the U.S.A. and the U.S.S.R.

210)   *Establishing New Priorities.* Focusing national energies and budgets on acquiring weapons makes it almost impossible to give adequate attention to social development initiatives for alleviating the human misery in much of the world. On the contrary, such a skewed sense of national priorities greatly contributes to those conditions. The U.S. Catholic Bishops in their pastoral letter on peace declare that such "a massive distortion of resources in the face of crying human need creates a moral question." The Sixth Assembly of the World Council of Churches declared from Vancouver, Canada in 1983: "Science and technology, which can do so much to feed, clothe, and house all people, can today be used to terminate the life of the earth. The arms race everywhere consumes great resources that are desperately needed to support human life." New strategies to care for human needs and to deal with the cause of unrest and conflict are therefore imperative. The role of the nation in international relations surely involves extending the general global welfare fully as much as protecting freedom by force of arms.

211)   *Openness, Honesty, and Respect for Others.* It is time for powerful nations, especially those which speak as champions of the free world, to renounce duplicity, covert operations, and secret wars. Such strategies are shortsighted and self-defeating. It is time also to abandon our too frequent disregard for world opinion and our refusal to take seriously the concerns of smaller nations except as they coincide with our own. Much too commonly the superpowers use their influence in small nations to prop up friendly authorities, even though these do not reflect the will of the people in those nations. Consider Afghanistan, Grenada, Poland, Vietnam, and others. Most of all, it is time for a new international understanding of security as equally important for all people everywhere, for ours is an interdependent world.

212)   *The U.S. Institute for Peace.* The 98th Congress established a U.S. Institute for Peace, embodying many of the purposes of the Peace Academy bill. While the peace institute is not a degree-granting institution, it is empowered to channel funds into peace studies and activities designed to develop constructive ways of managing international conflict, reducing the incidence of violence, and promoting a more peaceful world. Efforts must continue to upgrade the status of the institute and to expand its potential for implementing more effective strategies for resolving conflict without resort to violence. Particularly crucial to the launching of the enterprise is the provision of adequate funds and the appointment of aggressive leadership. Evidence of strong popular demand for underwriting this program will be necessary to assure a significant role for the institute, especially in this time of grave concern over deficits in the federal budget.

213)   *A New Attitude Toward National Sovereignty.* Equally important as such an institutional effort at peacemaking is the development of a new attitude toward national sovereignty. Since the late Middle Ages most people have taken it for granted that it is proper for a nation to do what is right in its own eyes. Popular opinion and national practice alike regard nation-states as their own arbiters of right and wrong. The development of institutions for serving the cause of world order, justice, and freedom has made little headway as yet against the absolutizing of national sovereignty. Yet in confessing Jesus Christ as Lord, Christians acknowledge that the nation is not ultimate nor the final judge of its own actions. The perils of a nuclear age, when the decision of one government may conceivably inflict destruction on all people, call for new and deeper reflection on limiting the claims of national sovereignty without imperiling the benefits which free nations have secured for their people.

3. The Church as Peacemaker
214)   In a world endangered by the threat of nuclear annihilation and pulled apart by opposing political ideologies, gross economic inequities, and polarizing rhetoric, the church is called to be reconciler and peacemaker. The church is not limited by political boundaries; it transcends national identities in celebrating the unity of the human family in God's creation.

215)   Historically involved in social mission and overseas ministries, churches now perceive the need for a new emphasis on worldwide reconciliation, service, and witness which extends beyond the countries of their traditional missionary activities. Mission education study themes and people-to-people programs that encourage greater understanding of the Soviet Union are examples of this. Within the global ecumenical community church people promote international dialogue on many human concerns, thus encountering varied perspectives on the problems of the world and their solution. Not only for communication at such meetings, but also as a prime means of understanding other peoples and their cultures, learning to speak a second language is a valuable skill; unfortunately, many Canadians and Americans have neglected to develop it.

216)   The church is keeper of a great tradition of pleading for justice and peace. Time and again since the days of Jesus and the martyrs, the faithful witness of a few of God's faithful people has thwarted the powers of this world, despite their political authority and military might. Here is an aspect of our common Christian calling particularly emphasized in pacifism, which should not be limited to the small minority of principled pacifists within the church. It is the positive, nonviolent effort to correct injustices before they result in an outbreak of hostilities. Economic independence, self-determination, and political freedom were specific goals of nonviolent movements led by Mahatma Gandhi (who was greatly influenced by Jesus) and Martin Luther King, Jr. These movements proved more effective deterrents to open conflict than the buildup of arms and preparation for war. The civil rights movement has drawn strength from a fundamental, uncompromising commitment to the principle of nonviolence. In the struggle against segregation in the United States, when many persons, black and white, were eager for an opportunity to do the right thing, an appeal to morality prevailed. This dimension of our Christian heritage calls for new initiatives by the church.

217)   Churches everywhere are speaking out as advocates for justice and peace in the world. The pastoral letter on peace by the U.S. Conference of Catholic Bishops has prompted other church groups, including Disciples, to grapple with issues of war and peace in the nuclear age. From Vancouver the World

Council of Churches sounded a clear Christian call: "The biblical vision of peace with justice for all, of wholeness, of unity for all God's people is not one of several options for the followers of Christ. It is an imperative in our time."[27] In 1982 a world conference hosted by the Russian Orthodox Church, with the theme of "saving the sacred gift of life from nuclear catastrophe," declared, "Peace should not be separated from justice for all; only a just peace can prevail."[28]

218)   The linkage of the cause of justice and peace is emphatically affirmed in Resolution 8148, which set the priorities for Disciples in the past quadrennium. Disciples have made a commitment to the pursuit of peace with justice, acknowledging that "the biblical imperative of peace, along with the justice that makes it possible, is at the heart of the Christian gospel. Making peace and therefore being among the blessed is a teaching of Jesus that applies in the congregation, in the region, in the nation, in the world. It is inextricably interwoven with hunger and human rights concerns and is linked to a congregation's life and witness. It means dealing with questions of control of nuclear power, armaments, peace-keeping mechanisms based on the equality and oneness of nations under God, crime, injustice, systemic violence, revolution, freedom, racism, discrimination, and economic inequality. World peace is a prerequisite for any improvement in the living conditions of the world's people." New redemptive ministries in pursuit of peace are therefore a priority for the church.

219)   It seems all too clear that a preoccupation with the building up of military strength has distorted national priorities. The church is called upon to condemn the injustices caused by that distortion and to lift up continually the vision of God's *shalom*, giving witness to the essential interdependence of all of God's creation, especially of the human family. As urgent as it is to keep our world from being consumed by nuclear fire, the corollary need to work for more just relations among peoples and to overcome the misery which threatens the existence of much of humanity today, also demands our attention. True peace cannot be built on a foundation of injustice.

220)   Confronted by the awesome magnitude of the nuclear threat, we find no ready-made, simple solution. The widespread prevalence of injustice, economic exploitation, hunger,

and political terrorism across the world combines with the threat of nuclear holocaust to call the church to bold new ventures in the mission of peacemaking laid upon us by our Lord. Our temptation is to ignore this challenge or to refuse to grapple openly and courageously with the reality of our ethical predicament. The Panel urges every reader to reject all such temptations and respond affirmatively to the "Call to Commitment" sounding in the present hour. Our understanding of God and of the realities of our world demands our dedicated effort as Christians to make peace while there is yet time.[29]

A Call to Commitment

221)   Amid the sound and fury of all the new weapons and all the old angers every Christian heart is summoned to be a maker of peace. Although we are tempted to ignore the call to peacemaking, we do not have the option to refuse the challenge. Our faith demands that we respond as individuals and as a church with daring new vision and bold new ventures for the making of peace.

222)   Our resolve to heed that call carries us into the moral reaches of our faith in search of a clearly charted course toward peace. But the nuclear threat, born of the technology of our day, has spawned moral questions unprecedented in their complexity. Moral dilemmas confront us at every turn and in our pursuit of that world in which no sword is drawn we find ourselves pulled in many directions at the same time. It is ultimately through Jesus the Christ, the fulfillment of *shalom*, that we find our way. With his teachings as compass, every disciple is fully able to set a daring course toward peace, a course of new vision and new venture through the moral tangle of the nuclear age.

223)   The course that we set should lead us toward human community and away from war, that ancient institution of national interest which is humankind's oldest and most dreaded scourge. "War," asserts a recent Nobel laureate, "paves the road to peace with human bones."[30] The threat of war will continue to overshadow the planet until humanity is able to see that above all the tribes and all the nations is the human family, the sisterhood and brotherhood of all people, until we are able to see our wholeness and common destiny with more clarity than we see our divisions and differences. Part of the new vision and

new venture will be the recognition that we are all "members one of another" (Ep 4:25). Only then can we break down the barriers of mistrust which thwart our best insights and highest resolves toward a human community at peace.

224)   At the heart of our new vision and new venture on the course toward peace will be Jesus the Christ. His way of love is infinitely more powerful than the way of war and violence. "Returning violence for violence multiplies violence, adding deeper darkness to a night already devoid of stars. Darkness cannot drive out darkness; only light can do that. Hate cannot drive out hate; only love can do that."[31] Yet humankind still clings to the ancient fallacy which claims that we can use force to rearrange the external political configurations and thus the wrongs of the world will be set right. Instead of tinkering with these surface externals, Jesus the Christ attacks evil in its breeding place—the heart of humanity: the hearts of nations, the hearts of institutions, and the hearts of persons. Here is supremely the place where the church must focus its vision. Weapons of war are set to their task by the human hand, but the hand is set to its task by the human heart. Thousands of years of human experience have proved over and over again that the heart of all transformation is the transformation of the heart.

225)   Take up the challenge! Become a maker of peace! Work and pray for reconciliation wherever misunderstanding, suspicion, and enmity prevail. Engage others in your church and community in study, dialogue, and action to prevent a resort to arms. Put yourself to the hard task of making up your mind about specific issues of nuclear policy. Then use your influence to change public opinion and to influence governmental decisions. Dare to set your course toward the wholeness of the human family at peace and be bold enough to chart that course with faithful witness to Christ's way of love, justice and peace. For that way is *shalom*.

Panel on Christian Ethics in a Nuclear Age

Eugene W. Brice, Kansas City, Missouri
D. Duane Cummins, St. Louis, Missouri
Newton B. Fowler, Jr., Lexington, Kentucky
Kenneth E. Henry, Atlanta, Georgia
Jane W. Hopkins, Los Angeles, California
JoAnne H. Kagiwada, Indianapolis, Indiana
Thomas J. Liggett, Indianapolis, Indiana
Ronald E. Osborn, Seaside, Oregon
Kenneth L. Teegarden, Indianapolis, Indiana

Notes

1. Geoffrey R. Nuttall, *Christian Pacifism in History* (Oxford: Blackwell, 1958), pp. 27, 41.

2. Charles Earle Raven, *The Theological Basis for Christian Pacifism* (New York: Fellowship Publications, 1951), p. 25.

3. Robert McAfee Brown, *Making Peace in the Global Village* (Philadelphia: Westminster Press, 1981), p. 41.

4. William W. Rankin, *The Nuclear Arms Race* (Cincinnati: Forward Movement Press, 1981), pp. 86, 87.

5. Roland H. Bainton, *Christian Attitudes Toward War and Peace* (New York: Abingdon Press, 1960), p. 115.

6. Ibid., p. 111.

7. "Address on War" (Wheeling, Va., 1848), pp. 348-356, in Alexander Campbell, *Popular Lectures and Addresses* (Philadelphia: James Challen & Son, 1863).

8. W. B. Blakemore, "Reasonable, Empirical, Pragmatic: The Mind of Disciples of Christ," *The Reformation of Tradition*, edited by Ronald E. Osborn (St. Louis: The Bethany Press, 1963), p. 174.

9. The thesis of this section is advanced by William H. McNeill, *The Pursuit of Power* (Chicago: The University of Chicago Press, 1983), especially pp. 69, 117, 131-154.

10. *Effects of Nuclear War: An Official U.S. Appraisal* (Washington: The Office of Technical Assessment of the United States Congress, 1979).

11. Jonathan Schell, *The Fate of the Earth* (New York: Alfred A. Knopf Press, 1982).

12. Walter Brueggemann, *Living Toward a Vision: Biblical Reflections on Shalom* (Philadelphia: United Church Press, 1976), p. 15.

13. Stephen Charles Mott, *Biblical Ethics and Social Change* (New York: Oxford University Press, 1982), p. 168.

14. National Conference of Catholic Bishops, *The Challenge of Peace: God's Promise and Our Response*, p. 18.

15. Message from the Sixth Assembly of the World Council of Churches, *Gathered for Life* (Grand Rapids: Wm. B. Eerdmans Publishing Co., 1983), p. 3.

16. The title of a sermon by the youthful Alexander Campbell.

17. For a notable discussion of the living God of compassion and wrath, see Abraham J. Heschel, *The Prophets* (New York: Harper & Row, Publishers, 1962), chaps. 12-18.

18. Daniel Day Williams, *God's Grace and Man's Hope* (New York: Harper & Row, Publishers, 1949).

19. Jonathan Schell, "Reflections: The Abolition," *The New Yorker*, Jan. 2, 1984, p. 37.

20. Willard M. Swartley, *Slavery, Sabbath, War and Women* (Scottdale, Pa.: Herald Press, 1983).

21. James Russell Lowell, text for "Once to Every Man and Nation."

22. Alexander Campbell, *The Millennial Harbinger*, Jan. 4, 1830.

23. James A. Crain, *The Development of Social Ideas Among the Disciples of Christ* (St. Louis: The Bethany Press, 1969).

24. See William D. Hartung, *The Economic Consequences of the Nuclear Freeze* (New York: Council on Economic Priorities, 1984).

25. See Department of Church in Society, *Memorandum:...The Official Statements and Resolutions of the Christian Church (Disciples of Christ) Regarding Conscientious Objection to War and Military Service* (Indianapolis: Division of Homeland Ministries, 1983).

26. The Declaration of Independence.

27. "Statement on Peace and Justice," Sixth Assembly of the World Council of Churches, *Gathered for Life*, p. 132.

28. "An Appeal to the Leaders and Followers of All Religions," World Conference of Religious Workers for Saving the Sacred Gift of Life from Nuclear Catastrophe, Moscow, U.S.S.R., May, 1982.

29. Some of the ideas in this section are elaborated in the documents cited in the notes and in the following: Edward Leroy Long, Jr., *Peace Thinking in a Warring World* (Philadelphia: The Westminster Press, 1983); Ruth Leger Sivard, *World Military and Social Expenditures 1983* (New York: World Priorities, 1983).

30. Jaroslav Seifert, *The Casting of Bells* (Iowa City, Ia.: The Spirit That Moves Us Press, 1984), p. 51.

31. Lines from the writings of Martin Luther King, Jr. as cited in *The Idea of Disarmament: Rethinking the Unthinkable* by Alan Geyer (Elgin, Ill.: The Brethren Press, rev. ed., 1985), p. 216.

Resources for Study

Basic Information on Major Themes

The Effects of Nuclear War, published by Office of Technology Assessment, Congress of the United States, 1979 (may be ordered from The Sycamore Community, P.O. Box 1325, State College, PA 16801, $3.00).

A collaborative investigation by the Department of Defense, the Central Intelligence Agency, the Arms Control and Disarmament Agency, and the Congressional Research Service, this book makes a comparative study of the probable effects of a nuclear attack on major cities of the U.S.S.R. and the U.S.A., using Detroit and Leningrad as case studies, and attempts to project the long-term effects of nuclear war.

Living Toward a Vision: Biblical Reflections on Shalom, by Walter Brueggeman (United Church Press, 1982, $6.95).

A fresh and relevant approach to one of the major themes of scripture, this study by a thoroughly prepared biblical scholar develops the fullness of the concept of *shalom*, which our document can only briefly suggest; this book has won a wide influence in religious circles.

Gathered for Life, edited by David Gill (Eerdmans Publishing Co., 255 Jefferson Ave. SE, Grand Rapids, MI 45903, 1984, $12.95).

The official report of the Sixth Assembly of the World Council of Churches, held in Vancouver, Canada, 24 July-10 August, 1983, the book narrates the major events of that gathering, and presents the text of addresses and reports dealing with the theme: "Jesus Christ, the Life of the World."

The Challenge of Peace: God's Promise and Our Response, by the National Conference of Catholic Bishops (Paulist Press, 1983, $1.50).

An analysis of the nuclear threat in terms of the Catholic moral tradition, especially in the light of the just war theory, the pastoral letter is comprehensive, well reasoned, clear, and empirically informed; it is required reading for anyone concerned with ethical aspects of nuclear war.

The Idea of Disarmament: Rethinking the Unthinkable, by Alan Geyer (The Brethren Press, rev. ed., 1985, $11.95).

This comprehensive, scholarly examination of the issues of nuclear disarmament exposes the futility of the arms race, challenges the religious and secular communities to exercise greater influence in the matter, and proposes a realistic strategy.

The Nuclear Delusion: Soviet-American Relations in the Atomic Age, by George F. Kennan (Pantheon Books, 201 E. 50th St., New York, NY 10022, 1982, $13.95).

A careful review of American-Soviet relationships, the book analyzes strategic objectives, detente, and the nuclear arms race, concluding with a reasoned and eloquent plea for the abandonment of nuclear weapons on the grounds that a nuclear arms race is simply unnecessary.

Selected Readings

Christian Attitudes Toward War and Peace, Roland H. Bainton, Abingdon, 1960.
The Countdown to Disaster, William W. Rankin, Forward Movement Publication, 1981.
The Fate of the Earth, Jonathan Schell, Knopf, 1982.
Hunger for Justice, Jack A. Nelson, Orbis, 1980.
Nevertheless: The Varieties of Religious Pacifism, John H. Yoder, Herald Press, 1972.
New Call for Peacemakers, Maynard Shelly, Faith and Order Press, 1979.
Peace Is Possible: A Study/Action Process Guide on Peacemaking, Shirley J. Heckman, United Church Press, 1982.